Sticks and Stones

A memoir by Paul Scrase

Sticks and Stones
A memoir by Paul Scrase

© 2016 Paul Scrase

ISBN 9780993526541

First published in 2016 by Arkbound Ltd (Publishers)

■■■

Arkbound is a social enterprise that aims to promote social inclusion, community development and artistic talent. It sponsors publications by disadvantaged authors and covers issues that engage wider social concerns.

Arkbound fully embraces sustainability and environmental protection. It endeavours to use material that is renewable, recyclable or sourced from sustainable forest.

Arkbound
Backfields House
Upper York Street
Bristol BS2 8QJ
England

www.arkbound.com

Contents

<u>Chapter 1 – Early Days</u>

As I write this book I have a warrant out for my arrest.

My beginning was not much different to a lot of other people's, I suppose. I was a spring baby born on the 29th of April 1965. Given what I ended up doing, you might think I came from rough beginnings. But I didn't. I had a good upbringing with two sisters and parents in a stable marriage, who are still with us now.

I went to school at Ashton Vale – then the Ashton Gate schools, Ashton Park Lower School and Ashton Park Upper School. I was far from a model student: my spelling was shit and my English was worse. Out of school I did normal kids' stuff – stream jumping, den building. My mother and father always gave their heart and soul to family life and I know that I was a constant worry to them.

At Ashton Vale things were pretty good really. I went to a boys' club and learned to fight, to play football and box. I loved chilling out with my mates and discovered the allure of the opposite sex very early. It probably started with me chasing them or them chasing me although there was one special girl then, Caroline; but I was too young (around 11 years old) to do much about it. I do remember having holidays with her family and her coming with my family on holiday too.

I developed a healthy interest in money early on as well. I got myself a window-cleaning job around the age of 11 with a mate called Cockney Mike, and suddenly I had loads of 50ps jangling in my pocket. Another venture was inspired by the fact that I lived near fields where horses were kept: I used to collect horse manure and sell it to keen gardeners. *Where there is muck there is brass*, as they say up North!

I was never a fan of the police; it was a dislike that started when I got a belting round the head by one of them for smoking. I had them down as bullies.

Then there was the time I got the blame for slashing the tyres on the lady next door's car. It seemed I was always branded as big trouble and I pretty much lived up to this reputation.

The peak of my success was setting fire to a factory and then blowing it up. The feeling I got from watching those flames devour the building was like no other. I felt a need to explore what fire could do; what power it had; what destruction it could cause – to people and buildings. Into my teens, I became only too familiar with its awesome power.

Although I have never been into watching football, I liked the five-aside games that we played at the boys' club in Ashton. In those days it kept a lot of bad lads like me occupied for some of the time. And of course, where there are boys there will be girls and more grief. I was always in trouble of one sort or another!

So there I was with my own little moneymaking empire that I had worked hard for and a good family, married parents, and two sisters who I loved to bits. But outside the four walls of my happy home I would meet up with my mates: the good, the bad, and the butt-fucking ugly. Despite it all I got 7 solid GCSE's, God knows how! I have a vague memory of those poor souls who tried to keep me contained during school hours: Mr Radford, Miss Keene and old Jack House – a devout Bristol City fan.

Then there was Ian. Like me, he had an affinity with breaking into property. Factories, shops, caravans – you name it, if we could break into it, we did. Our first 'job' was the cricket club that was beside our school. We decided we would take the afternoon off school. I was 13 by this time and very keen to get my hands on money, one way or another. I was growing up and getting bolder. Looking back now I suppose there are a lot of things that I am sorry about in my life...

Inevitably we were nicked and found ourselves nailed to the floor in a fucking police station, with me in court at the age of 13! I stood there, a hard-faced magistrate looking down on me, directing the probation service to supervise me. It was probably a timely intervention in the run-up to leaving Ashton Park Upper School.

Sticks and Stones

Alongside this world of crime and probation was my first proper girlfriend. She was a very stunning young lady and is still stunning to this day, I am told. With her positive influence, I ended up getting into scaffolding – a world of sheer graft. But hard work didn't bother me so I had an interview with a large firm, and they agreed to take me on. The only condition was that I had to do a year in college first, which meant leaving behind my girlfriend. It was hard for me. I am not a soft person, but every man loves and wants to be loved. Young love is a fragile thing and with me away our relationship eventually faded.

My mother tells me that those college days were a turning point and marked the point where I began to go really wrong.

I met some good blokes there and some right wankers too. It was 1982 at the Kings Lynn Bircham Newton Construction Industry Training Board site. It used to be an old airfield and we were billeted in the old H blocks in dormitories. There was a lot there: a swimming pool, gym, cinema... and of course work in the daytime. It was one of the best construction colleges in the world.

I finished the course and was catapulted back into the world of scaffolding for the firm who had paid for my year in college. It was hard work and poor pay, but it was a job. I had been earning more cleaning windows when I was 11! Eventually

I jumped ship and went to another firm, SGB. By now things had begun to move and wages were a little better. They were a good bunch of men on the firm and we had good crack. I think some of those men have passed on, a road we all have to take – some too soon.

Needless to say, with my hard work, SGB had their money's worth out of me. One night I had worked overtime, fulfilled the task, and was moving towards getting home. The supervisor gave me the nod to take one of the company's large transit vans. *All cool*, I thought. I had got a date with the scrap man's daughter so I was in a rush to get home and have tea – shit, shave, shower and dress for a rocking night in the van! Off I went around the pubs, the Black Horse – in those days called The Old Cider House – where only twenty people made it seem crowded. Then it was on to meet the scrap man's daughter.

By now I had drunk a skinful and was driving the van with a good-looking girl, although in this case beauty was probably in the eye of the beholder. But with my beer goggles on I had one thing on my mind, and it was not a fucking curry I was after! We had got into a bit of a crash on an A road and I went straight to it, my face buried between my date's legs, totally oblivious to the fact that we were blocking the road with no room for traffic. I had gone for the muff diving as an attempt to warm her up, but all I could think of was to get it over and get me in!

It was about three in the morning.

Eventually we were given a lift to a phone box, but by that time someone had rung the Old Bill. They pulled up with the woman who had seen me crash the van in the back of the cop car.

"You are nicked, son," one particularly punchable pig said.

"Oh fuck!" I responded. "Let my mother know what is going on!"

I had learnt not to grass anyone, so I took the rap for the van. I told the filth that I took it without permission. I would never have told them that the supervisor had said I could take it. This is the first lesson: *do the crime and be willing to do the time*. That is in the back pages of the bible or somewhere! Apparently our Lord will forgive you.

Thanks to this incident, I was out of work and on my way to prison for the first time at the age of 20. They sent me to a young offenders' prison in Weymouth. I ended up in one of the units called Hardy House for 6 months and that hurt a lot, not knowing what I would be up against and always worrying about money. But somehow I got a job as the gym orderly – taking over from a major player in there called Grant. So now I was in it up to my fucking neck!

Every day we had to make our beds neatly and clean our boots for inspection. I met a friend there, Dave, whom I knew from Bristol. He showed me how to survive in prison. Then finally I was given my release date: two days before my 21st birthday.

Out again, back on the bumpy road of life. Although I had dreaded it, prison was pretty easy. I came out a free man... but with no job, no regime to stick by, and little support. For the first time in my life I went to sign on.

Bizarrely the Old Bill asked me to do an identification parade up the nick and paid me for it, so at least I got some money! I think they paid 8 pounds – a much needed top up to the jobseekers' allowance!

Shortly after I had a call from the area manager from the firm I had just been to prison for 'stealing' from. *Would you like to start back?* he asked.

Oh yes! It was the one thing I knew how to do: work hard. So back I went. It was great being back amongst the banter at work again, and now I was earning proper money and the world was my oyster.

I met someone special too, a girl on my arm that I loved.

I had also been handed a deal of a lifetime. Whilst in prison my father bought about 25 lorry loads of scaffolding kit for – wait for it – the princely sum of £25.00! Surely I would earn a place in the Guinness Book of Records for that. There was one fly in the ointment: I took my second cousin on board.

I got married to the girl I loved. At first we were really happy, and we had a beautiful daughter who we named Portia Faye. I was over the moon: Portia was the light of my life, from the minute I laid eyes on her. She always was and always will be. I had wanted to give everything to her mother, but in a pattern that was to repeat itself through my life, I fucked it up. I was living it large: far too much money, a little fucked in the head, a dare devil on the scaffolding.

Back then, at the age of 23 and with Portia on the way, I sold gear to buy our first house. I would have given my wife anything, but money can't buy love – or can it? Anyway, looking back, that first house in Barton Hill was a shithole – although I suppose it was OK for 25 years ago.

So here I was with my first house and a baby on the way. I was working for a scaffolding company where my boss was a complete bastard of a man! Someone had told him that I had been 'stealing' his scaffolding gear. Well, for once the finger was pointed at the wrong person. But this twat went to see my wife on a Sunday afternoon. When I was working for him in Cheddar he just decided to pop round to my house. I think he planned to rape my wife while he knew I was busy working for him.

It was not until he did that, went to my home and frightened the life out of my wife, that just maybe I might have started to take his scaffolding kit. I even rang him and told him I was coming to see him. I lost that job but I got the money he owed me for 9 days: £450.00 to the penny.

At that time, I was just going from job to job. People said I would steal anyone's kit, but that wasn't true. One firm in particular comes to mind, owned by a big-mouth owner with seriously bad habits. One day he got a visit from the rightful owners of the gear he had nicked. They turned up with lorries, wielding a big stick or two. The cowardly owner shit himself. The blokes that showed up were from out of town and quite big in the boxing world. He had to give their kit back and plenty more of his own to boot.

Now that's what I call a lesson.

Chapter 2 – Love and Marriage

So I was married with a baby girl – Portia Faye Scrase. From the first minute I set eyes on her, my heart was lost to her, and still is. I had all any man could want. But the problem was that when I am with a woman – although I don't think they belong to me – I have Taurus for my birth sign and can be a very jealous man. Sometimes that jealousy manifests itself in a good way and other times not so much. In my mind the girl of my dreams should have anything she wants and in a way, at least at first, she did.

I was working hard in scaffolding with a man in Chew Valley, just outside of Bristol. Chew Valley is a lovely part of the country, but I was about to learn that there are rogues everywhere, even at local beauty spots! We formed a firm with me doing all the scaffolding for him. He had a roofing firm so I was as happy as a pig in shit.

For a few years everything went well. We had moved into our second home and had rented out the old place so were flying. But, at the same time, my drinking was increasing and we were not really making ends meet. I also realised that I was being ripped right off. Coming from a good family, one thing I will not tolerate is being ripped off! I asked this man for the accounts so we could have a look at the books. I thought that we needed a second opinion.

When we came to collect the books, he gave me some bullshit that they were not ready. I had my wife and Portia Faye with me so we had a meeting with their accountant. He told me: "if you don't understand money, then don't be in business!"

This led me to start asking questions about the money situation. When I first went into partnership, I had had five thousand in the bank and I wanted to know where that was now. It had also been suggested that my partner's stepson be taken on board. But one thing I didn't need was a spy in the cab, or rather the lorry. There was already one tachograph telling me I couldn't drive, or telling me I'd done too many hours, and so on. So how, with no money coming in, were we going to pay for another man doing 14 or 16 hours a day all week?

I am pretty well known in old Bristol for lots of different reasons. Going into business was a pretty steep learning curve. I was working like a field hand, harder than I had ever worked. But this was an opportunity, an open chequebook and a chance to earn decent money. For once in my life I was going straight. Another first: I went on a weekend break with my wife, leaving the baby safely at home with my mother.

It was like being on honeymoon: we could not stay away from one another all the way down and all the way back. I loved this girl to bits I would have given her anything. Here I was: a shotgun wedding, a family... and a scaffolding firm that was not making money.

While I was away, I had men working for me, or so I thought. At the place where we were working, you had to take a shower after the work because it was a black shit hole to work in. It turned out that the men let me down all weekend. There were no mobiles then – good in one way but not in another because when I got home I had about 15 messages telling me to move the scaffolding kit off site and giving me 24 hours to do so! The firm now told me to take them to court for my money – things could not have been worse. For all that, I can tell you one thing: for all the grief it caused me, I would not have missed that weekend away for anything. I loved it and I loved her.

* * *

I had an old friend at the time, Mr Meacham. He was a sound bloke but never liked the hours I worked. I can remember working until midnight then going to pick up the last load of gear on site, so maybe he had a point! Now you have to remember I had been dealt a short hand again on money – I was owed around £23k. One man said no to me, so to cause him some damage we rang his wife to tell her he was having an affair. The girl I got to call his wife was very convincing on the phone. That was fair enough, I thought, since he had fucked my life!

But things were not going well in my own marriage and it felt as though my whole life was falling apart. I was out drinking a lot, not really taking much on board. £23k was a lot of money to lose, as well as the money that I had already paid out to the men to earn that money in the first place. I was also doing lots of jobs for a firm called Kelsey roofing as well as lots of other people. There is only one option in scaffolding: do it right, or don't do it at all. One job comes to mind as an example of what can go wrong, with the whole lot falling over into the street because the roofer had mixed up the tiles. Luckily it missed all the cars that were parked but it took out every BT phone line in the street.

I was always up for cheap scaffolding kit because I knew that if I didn't have it someone else would. An old friend decided to pass a load of scaffolding kit on to me that had just been taken from a site in Bristol. When I say a "site" I mean their yard – don't worry, not from a small firm but from a very large one who could afford to take the hit! So I bought lots of 'bones' – a term we use in Bristol for scaffolding. I ended up with a couple of garages full. I couldn't tell who had actually robbed the firm; often bones were just passed from one person to several others. But I don't grass – never have and never will.

At home we had a BMW, a nice house. But I always smashed the cars up and I smashed up the house now and again as well. I will always say sorry to someone I loved dearly. I carry a lot of burning candles for a lot of women I have been with. I've definitely got two candles burning – sorry, three, as I have one for Rita from Bristol. How could I forget you, young lady! This is a lady who has moved on in her life; she is stunning with great kids as well. Her boyfriend was killed in a drug deal. I often think of her and hope she is doing well.

With no money about I replaced the BMW with a black Fiat Panda. Things were going downhill fast and I was desperately trying to hold on to someone I loved dearly. Once, after we had a bust up, she was over at her mum's again so me and a friend popped over. The answer was no, I couldn't see her. I decided to get the pram out of car and smash all the windows in with it.

After I had finished, it was left hanging out of the windscreen.

When I think back to the time we lived in the flat, I was always losing it. Once I woke up to find the baby's high chair hanging out the window – Portia was not in the chair at the time, thank fuck!

I had a bit of a thing about windows. I used to get taxis now and again when I was out. Let's just say there is more than one story about pots of paint going through the window of the taxi or tins of tomatoes – I don't really know why, I really don't. So the high chair was another pissed up moment in my life.

The truth is that I am not a good drinker, I never have been. I went from the weed to the piss. I stopped smoking weed years ago after I lost a month's remission time in prison. But drink, despite its bad effects, was much harder to give up.

There are firms around that are trading on the wing of a prayer and then there are great firms I have worked for – Taylor scaffolding, now he was a man who could teach you all you needed to know. That firm has finished but he should have made it big time. It was some time ago that I worked for him.

"Go and buy some bones from the suppliers," he'd say and off we would go. We ended up with the bones on our lorry with another firm's name on them. It turned out that old Taylor knew the name and the owner so they got together by phone and made a deal. The lesson is: don't sell scaffolding kit to another firm with someone else's name – although if you did, it could be that you had a licence to buy any of their kit legally. I should know. I've been to court with it and got away with it. So all these firms that sell kit on with your name on it don't mean a wank – at the end of the day lots of scaffolding firms start up a bit dodgy. That is just the way it is!

I was splitting up with my business partner in my scaffolding business. He told me I was a working partner – he had lots of money but never drew a wage so my share of the business was worthless. He had bought into me, but never took out any money. It was a hard lesson to learn and I would advise anyone to never go into business with another person – even if you think you trust them.

But my biggest regret at that time was probably the fact that I had started a marriage and I had failed in a big way. I will never forget her; she really was all I'd ever wanted in life and in a way, all I ever had that was great and good. To this day I love this girl still and will never stop burning a candle for her – in all it took me nearly 8 years to come to terms with losing her and our marriage but eventually time moves on and so do we, but that candle is still very much alight!

During this time I was living in Kingswood, North Bristol, despite being from South Bristol. Really I will lay my hat anywhere to live, except Ashton Vale! We were all out on the piss in Kingswood high street – making hay while the sun shines. We popped in to the boozer where the crooks of Kingswood drink. In a scaffolding firm you get to know everyone else in the game and those boys I had sold scaffolding to.

I didn't like the crew that much. In fact, I didn't like them at all. It ended up with me arguing with one main player and there was an almighty fucking bust up – over what I am not sure, even to this day. So with this big fight going on I put one of the old phones around his head – the ones that you needed a dialling knob to carry the numbers around. It must have hurt – and trying to leave nearly cost me my life. I ended up in intensive care for 7 days and the old man thought he was going to have to bury me.

As I was now going my own way in scaffolding, I thought that to make things fair I would take what was mine. There was a man that I'd not seen in a long time and we planned to set up a business in Weston Super Mare. I was working hard to cover my losses and make a living.

Chapter 3 – Doing Time

Out on bail, I was on the piss one Sunday and I thought I would pop back to see my wife. Unfortunately, what greeted me was some bloke who had obviously just had a blowjob with his feet up in my front room.

You my friend have just made the wrong turn - a really wrong turn.

All I could see was his hair and glasses – the window was in between us. So I launched myself through the window to get to him and he left by the same window that I had arrived through.

He ended up with more than 70 stitches.

I didn't really blame my wife, the mother of my child – I had put her through so much. I camped up in the loft for one night; a tactic I picked up in my younger days when someone broke in over the road from mother's house and hid in the loft.

Yet it was only a matter of time before jail caught up with me. It was not all bad, though. While I was in there I met a lot of men – the good the bad. Some stole cars, others dealt drugs, but they were all pleading not guilty, your honour. It was all going all right until I ended up on 'G' wing, which happened to be full of murderers and rapists.

There was nothing else to do except get my head down. Every day, I could rub shoulders with someone that had taken a life or two. One man sticks in my mind. He had been given a life sentence for killing someone, and if you're interested I do think that life should mean life. This particular guy had killed his wife and of course he was not guilty. When he failed to persuade the jury to his way of thinking and he was found guilty, he had to be taken to the hospital wing. He probably ended up going to one of those high security mental hospitals, getting treatment rather than punishment.

So, there I was in the nick on the sewing machine making 100 towels a day – on top earner – and going down the gym now and again. I must say that, overall, Horfield prison was OK once you got used to choosing your food a day in advance.

Some time into my sentence I got a letter saying I had a baby on the way. I remember thinking – hey, don't I get a say in it? I even knew the young lady's old man. He should have put his foot down – I would never bring up anyone else's kids. I have tried that a few times and my opinion had been formed, fuck that! Next came a letter to say that my wife was divorcing me in jail.

To cap all this off, I was having to cope with a constant smell. Most of the lifers in nick are willing to take your life or the life of anyone else who looks at them the wrong way. Now I had to share my cell with one of them. He seemed to be taking a shit all the time, not like normal people who go in the morning for the day. He stank the cell out, and the cell was not big, only 7ft x 12ft. He stank me up as well, and I had to shower every morning.

One day we saw a page of the Evening Post that reported some bastard robbing an old lady of her pension as she was coming out the post office. Someone else just took the wrong turn, I thought! He went on 'Rule 43' for his own protection – that was where all the kiddie fiddlers, the scum of the earth, were kept. This guy reckoned he could deal with anything that came his way. Well, he had to deal with not one or two guys but more like four or five if I remember rightly, beating him with pool cues and batteries in socks. Topping if off was the jug of boiling water with a bag of sugar in it tipped over his head - hot and sticky, so it clings to the skin. Now that's got to hurt.

What did the screws do? Fuck all, as it all happened on 'association', which we had every other night. I was out of it but I had to get a jug of water for my night's cup of tea and I saw it all go off. I was told to fuck off back to my cell but I liked what I saw. In nick if someone deserves a good kicking then a blind eye is generally turned, and I think robbing an old lady is pretty much up there. The poor lady got robbed in my area too – in the Banjo Island area near to Kingswood. Well, lady, I know you lost your pension but at least the scumbag got properly dealt with!

You can make jail hard or easy for yourself. When I was first in jail in Weymouth I met a bloke called Dave and he taught me a lot about survival in nick. I remember the day that this screw called Scrase came in shouting his big fat fuck face off.

"Who the fuck in here is Paul Scrace?"

The door nearly came out of the stonewall it was fixed to.

"Me" I said.

He went mental. "Call me sir!" he yelled.

Because I was young he made it his mission to bully me and he had real issues with me being there and having the same surname as him. But he was nothing to me and I would rather be dead than his son or any relative, or the son of any screw.

In prison you do what you can to make things easier on yourself and getting a cell of my own would have made a massive difference. So when one night a screw handed me a mop and told me that a cell needed cleaning out, and in return I'd get to keep it myself, I jumped at the chance.

Off I went to my new cell. When I arrived, it looked like a scene from a horror movie. There was blood everywhere: on the floor, up the walls, fucking everywhere! Turns out that the bloke tried to top himself, so he was put on the hospital wing to be looked after. He was a big bloke too – he just couldn't do the time, or perhaps he was going to be someone's toy for the next few months and couldn't face that prospect, who knows!

One Sunday morning I was having a quick wash in my cell standing there in a vest and boxers when a big motherfucker came in my cell. Now this boy is doing life and he has fuck all to lose!

He asked me if I had been borrowing on his patch. Borrowing means earning on the inside. He thought I was selling drugs on his wing. I thought my time was up. He had shut the door behind him.

I told him that I was borrowing tobacco – just two roll ups for a bar of soap, that sort of thing. He must have been convinced because he pressed the bell and the screws let him out. They had known that he was in with me, and turned a blind eye. I nearly shat myself. I thought that the Lord was looking down on me, and that's not the only day the Lord has looked down on me and saved my sorry white arse - God Save the Queen!

If there was a lot of gay activity in prison then I was not really aware of it. It is not like what you see on TV in the USA, full on blokes and all that. I'm not saying it doesn't go on behind cell doors. Men up doing life maybe? Who knows, but I think in jail it's done more on the quiet. I've done the nicks, slopping out sitting on a potty in the cell in the days when there were no shit houses in the cells. I sometimes think my life will come back and haunt me. I have never been a yes man for anything; I would never have got on in the army or any of the other forces.

* * *

I don't know if I will ever go to jail again. No man can say he will never go to jail; life has strange twists and turns. And then there are men who love the place for the three meals a day and in-cell TV. I've got a mate who has just been done and is back inside. Now I think he's going to grow old in there – he's up now for firearms. They found about 10k in his house too. Going in and out of jail is not worth the shit unless you know you're getting away with something big. Funny though, even now I make my bed every day – hungover or not – from the time I made bed packs in nick.

On release, I decided it was time to give up scaffolding and start using my HGV licence. I bought a fucking great big lorry in order to start moving rubbish for loss adjusters who sort out things for the insurance people. One of the first jobs was to clear up someone's garage that got burnt down by some lads. It brought back memories of my earlier years; I had set a few fires in my time. I got to the address in a suburb of Bristol to start work. The job was on a narrow lane at the back of a row of houses.

I took down the garage and loaded the lorry, ready to take the lot to the tip in the morning. Off I went when suddenly the back end of the lorry crashed into a garden. I tried to get out of there, only to see I was in another garden. Now I was stuck in two back gardens with an 18-ton truck loaded to the gunnels – I had never been shy on putting a load on a truck! I was stuck good and proper, in the fishpond too. I called a friend who had a wrecker, one of those big things that you see picking up a bus or towing a large truck. He came and got me out. Looking back at the damage to the back gardens, it was like a bomb site. I had to get away sharpish and I did not even send an invoice for the job. I was gutted, but life goes on.

For another job just outside of Bristol I didn't even get paid. When people don't pay how the fuck are you going to make your way?

I had lived in Ashton or Bedminster for a while and I got hired to clear a large area of waste, lots of it too, so I subbed it out. Now this was a job for some fat motherfucker, and when I say fat I mean he had a hard job even to walk. He had plenty of dosh mind you. He was a car dealer and everything was going well until the last payments – until, what do you know, he didn't pay up. The difference was this time I had to pay the sub-contractors I had hired. We eventually found his address and popped around to see him, but there was no one at home.

Well, this fucker looked like a real pervy bastard so we called around to the whorehouse. A jag was on the drive and the MOT, log book and fucking keys were left lying on a seat inside. *Lord, you keep looking down on me*, I am saying to myself. Off we go with the jag. I ring the fat bastard and ask for the money we're owed. Pay up or we'll sell the car, I tell him. Lo and behold, the money got sorted out.

I started to get to like this car game. The big crane on the back of my lorry started to look like a gold-miner.

I had been hanging around with a few lads who were in the mobile phone game on Winterstock road, and their neighbour was pissing them right off blocking their driveway all the time. They asked me to sort it so I went to pick the van up. It was a big fucking transit van, which I hauled off to the scrap yard. There were a few lads looking for a transit vans at the yard and they bought it from me. A nice little take.

Around this time they started applying the landfill tax, so I looked around to get a tip of my own on the principle that everything is possible. The tip that I ended up buying was a quarry – a large one and very deep too.

I picked up a job in Knowle West, where a house had burned down. The builder gave me the job to gut the house, so what couldn't be burned we tipped into the quarry. All the stuff we could burn went into the back garden. The son of the scrapyard owner was working for me and we were having a pint after the job when he looked up and said:

"We haven't set fire to that timber in the back garden."

We went back to light a fire and, as I have said, I have lit a few in my lifetime, but at this point I'd had a few drinks and I poured a lot of petrol all over the timber with rolled up paper and lit it.

Three seconds later my face became a ball of fire. The heat ripped through my flesh like someone pealing my face away with a Stanley knife.

I had never felt pain like that before. My mate took me to the police station across the road, one in Knowle that I had been to a few times before. They looked after me well, putting a facemask on with this special solution in it and getting me to hospital with second-degree burns. My head was like a rugby ball with skin hanging off.

It was not my finest hour.

Chapter 4 – The Name of the Game

I had lost my wife and child, and sadly I didn't see a lot of Portia Faye for many years. That is always something that I regret. On the work front I split from the Chew crew and then had a private investigator looking for me. "Why?" I asked at the time, "I only took what was mine." All the scaffolding was orange, so we re-painted it orange and blue but the funny thing was that the other side was orange and red – how bizarre was that? Some 80k had been spent on it and in the scaffolding game there is always a wrangle as to who owns what – it's not for the faint hearted.

My lorry was sold when I had a 'gypsies warning' from the mighty Mortimer Spike about the site where I had been tipping. He gave me a call to tell me I was being watched – I still have no idea who by. Spike was a local lorry mechanic – a fair man too. He has passed on now, and I am always sorry that I never got to say goodbye or farewell. I will never forget the big guy – Mighty Mortimer they called him, he got me out of some serious shit with the various lorries and trucks I've had over the years.

I worked for 'The Tailor' in Chew too – fuck me what an ugly man this boy was. He wanted a ride-on lawnmower. I got him one and then he cheated us on the money so we took it back a few months later just to prove a point. By this time I was getting pretty fed up with the 'bumping.' I have always earned good money but I've lost hundreds of thousands of pounds through people shafting me. Now I started to do jobbing work for lots of different firms and most people thought I was a rebel without a cause. I met up with a lad called Palmer, who I had done my training with, and Jeff Witcom – now there's a proper bloke too. I've seen lots going on in that firm and I've kept what I've seen to myself. I would never grass on anyone apart from a paedophile – all of whom, in my opinion, should be shot at point blank range. It makes me sick to think of people like that hiding their sick work – they need tarring and feathering instead of being sent to prison for a few months.

For the next while, anything that was not bolted down was fair game to be moved and sold by me.

When you're in prison, you get to know about people on the outside. I got some info on a man that used to 'ring' motors, although he had never been to jail and was now doing OK for himself in his own motor business specialising in lorries. Now this guy had tried to mess me up a long time ago and I thought I might pay him a visit. He had apparently had a plan to rob my generator out my van. What he did not know was that the generator was not in there because I had been doing the beer and fag runs from France at the time with my old mate Cockney Mike – a man you could trust.

I set up a cleaning company – Crystal Clear – steam cleaning lorries and doing some painting. I did the industrial cleaning with someone I will always love for the rest of my life, my father. He is someone I owe everything to – for standing by me – and my mother, who never gave up on me. I have met some great people in my life and a lot of hell raisers too. I've been told this book should be called 'Born to Raise Hell.' The thing is I don't think I was – it's just that I've had hell in my life.

I have had a lot of women in my life. It was cool back in the day and although I have no complaints about my sex life, I would still like to go back and visit some of those lovely ladies, sexy Donna and sexy Max. Ah, Maxine, she is a friend now but she was something else back in the day, fit was not the word. Oh, and Kelly who stole my TV! She broke into my sister's flat that I was renting from her at the time. Well, Kelly, I've got news for you: it wasn't my TV, girl. She was a little nuts that one!

Back to Maxine. Now she was a beautiful lady, with a mother in Canada. She was married to some idiot that was shitting on her, but she was close to her mother and her father, and he lived in this country. She wanted me to meet up with him to reassure him that I was OK. The reason that her folks were worried was because at that time I inhabited a world of whores and hookers, seedy flats and bed sits and a lot of stuff that goes on behind closed doors.

I went to meet Maxine's old man who was a big bloke. He had got information about me from her mother in Canada; someone had been filling her in on all the details. They did not have to worry about me going to Canada; my criminal record meant that I would not be welcome there or in the USA or Australia. Well that was Maxine, good memories. I met a lot of girls whose names escape me now, but at the time it was a lot of fun.

I was back living in Bedminster again by this time and good old Bedminster had come up in the world. It was quite a lovely place, a bit like lower Clifton. I was in my sister's flat – and I should take this chance to say sorry to her, although sis knows me; I will make money where I can. I had a lot to make up with all the bad luck or just not getting paid, but she was my sister and I do know that blood should be thicker than water.

I was still up to lots of shit, any shit I could get involved in really. One day I popped to the local corner shop for a paper and to look at the adverts in the window. One ad jumped out at me immediately. It was an advert asking for a broad-minded person. Well that's me, I thought. I was up for anything as long as I didn't have to dress up or wear high heels for a picture shoot, so I asked if I could take the advert out of the window. The shop was Pakistani owned and he told me that one of his relatives had another advert just like it down the road. So I bought both ads, left it for a day or two, then rang the number. A lady answered me and said she was looking to rent a bedroom on a long-term basis.

"Ok love," I said, "pop in and see me." Anyway we met and she was a dear old soul – Lucy Lou. She had a look around and asked me lots of things like was I around in the day? It was general chitchat really until she dropped the bombshell. She was a lady of the night, a hooker, a whore if you like – but what a woman with it! She was around 56 years of age and she had been at it all her life. She had worked in Bedminster for a long time and came from Mount Pleasant Terrace – a little hill in the same area, if I remember rightly. I happened to be in Vicarage Court, right next door to the church – on holy ground, I suppose!

Prostitution is a game that not many people would like to be in. Remember, I have a good father and mother who gave me a very good upbringing. But it was always MONEY with me. But let me tell you a little about these girls… probably more then you ever wanted to know, in fact.

I've always wondered what lead someone into prostitution and I was about to find out! There is a reason for everything in life and the lady of the night was paying me £300 a week to rent a room, which was a good enough reason for me! That's a lot of money – a touch over 15k a year on top of what I earned working. As I said, it was always the money with me; I didn't think much about what came with it, although one thing that does come with it is pretty girls.

I hung around for a while to see what it was all about and I've seen lots of things that never in my life would I like to be in or around. It works like this: you find a flat, rent it, put an advert in the paper for massage staff, and the phone starts to ring. When you find the staff you then put in another notice advertising the service. If you do 15 to 20 punters a day you will be earning around £400 a day. Now times that by 5 days a week and it makes 100k a year. That beats working for a living! If you have two or three places you can get 250k to 300k a year. Yet, what comes with the dark side of life is not all good.

The lady I mentioned stayed with me for nearly two years. She was never ever any trouble at all. She was what you call a pro in the game, and she had a good heart and soul. The old vicarage was rocking with 40 to 60 punters a week, sometimes 80 a week. A few even came back two or three times in the same week. I was amazed. How could people afford it?

My 'tenant' had two sons to bring up and I think she gave them the world and did everything she could. As well as that, she was also a very funny lady of the night. She ran like clockwork – never late, always the same hours. She was doing what she had to do or maybe even loved to do.

Things were good for a few months, then the lady who rented a flat downstairs died. I got a builder to move in on the place, someone who painted walls for a living. I thought I would rent that flat to another lady of the night and do the same thing.

Soon I had a house full of women on the game. I had met a girl called Karen, what a looker! She asked me to let her work in the place. "Ok let's do it!" I said. Once, when she was working on her own I hung around for a while. The phone goes and there is a punter outside who wants two girls. Luckily I did not have to put a dress on… but as we had no other girl, I had to have sex with her. He came in and I did my bit. The punter was a voyeur and I was not complaining; like I said, Karen was a very pretty girl. I got half of what she was paid, plus the house money!

I had got to know Lucy Lou pretty well by then and I was thinking of expanding my empire. Lucy was my breadwinner and I will say one thing about this lady – she was a fine lady of the night – or should that be day? A whore is not always someone who works only at night. Ladies of the night come in all shapes and sizes. Yes, there are some lovely lookers and some ugly ones too and ones that think they are too good to be in the game.

If you are reading this book and are thinking of going into the world of prostitution my advice to you would be to go and get a job in Tesco's or anywhere else. I will never understand a man letting his woman work as a whore. If you love that woman she wouldn't be doing that. My advice would be: never fall in love with a whore. Sadly, this book gets darker and darker by the chapter!

I decided to try expanding to Gloucester and I set off to find a place. It took no time to find a suitable property in Midland Road opposite the park. It was good to get away from Bristol where, despite the fact that it is a big city, people were starting to talk.

Perhaps you think it sounds pretty easy to run a whorehouse but remember one thing: you can go to jail for running whores. I was putting ads in the local papers that said *'girls wanted'*. The phone did not stop. So now I had a place in Gloucester as well as Vicarage Court in Bristol. Now you can't let the whores run the whorehouse as they will soon run your money away. I installed cameras and watched the videos back every week and picked up the dosh. I knew that without cameras I would not make a bean and the ladies would tell you that no one had been in. I was getting the hang of the whorehouse business. But there was more to come. Much more!

<u>Chapter 5 – Branching Out</u>

Now I was running a place in Gloucester but I had also taken on the green grocer's, complicated slightly by the fact that I didn't have a licence and had been banned around six times by this time. I had a lot of girls around when I branched out to Gloucester. Does that remind anyone of anything?

I was running the Vicarage Court site and the Gloucester house and I'd found a girl called Karen who moved in to look after the new place. But the thing is, however nice you think they are, they will fuck you over given half the chance.

I started to run adverts that covered Bristol and Gloucester. Things were slow at first but then they began to pick up. I was in Vicarage Court, although I was not living there anymore – I had rented a place in Temple Meads by the train station. It was very nice too, a three bed flat. A mate down from Newcastle had moved in to share the rent.

I had girls everywhere at that time, some even staying with us while they waited to go to Gloucester or The Vicarage, so we were flat out getting the right girls to the right places. I don't think I saw daylight for around two to three years over that time. A lot of them went into prostitution because they needed the money to study – life can make you do some very strange things, I learned.

One night a girl keen to start called up and arranged to meet her in a pub at Totterdown. She turned up and, believe me, she was to die for lads – I mean *to die for!* We were running late so Paki Bob took my place; he even said he was me, cheeky bugger! Well fuck me if he wasn't having a blowjob within ten minutes of meeting her. By the time I got there he was having a good laugh about it.

My mate *The Evening Post* – that's his nickname – went back to the flat to meet our newest recruit. I think there is probably an Evening Post in every city but he was always a good friend to me. Before I could put the tea on, the new girl was sucking The Post's cock then mine, then we were being fucked to within an inch of our lives!

At this time I was knocking off a bird in Stockwood – a working lady, need you ask, but a very fine fuck. We had got rid of the new girl who was totally insane and I wanted to take time out, open a bottle of wine, and chill. I was just beginning to relax when I got a call from my ex, the mother of my kids, telling me she had lost everything. Anyway the doorbell went and I didn't know who it was going to be: the Stockwood bird or the ex. How do you choose between someone you fuck and someone you once loved? Quid's in you choose love – always. I got her home and after a brief sex session, Stockwood went off with her tail between her legs. Now I am telling you I am up for most things, except a quiet life, and Bristol is a town where people love to talk.

So it was a farewell from my first wife. I remember that I had a call from my daughter once about her stepfather on a Sunday afternoon. I was out with the warlord Paul – a big time drug dealer – two tons of gear at a time in a horse trailer. I remember him telling me that it could take them two days to dig the stuff out of the trailer or horsebox – what a man! Next time we met I would be shaving his head for charity – mine as well. This was a man who knew how to live and there will be more about him later.

Following the call from my daughter I went up to Kingswood – I was pretty drunk, but I managed to get there and put the stepfather in his place. Next thing I know, he was calling the Old Bill, and at this stage I was way over the limit for drink driving. Like I said before, I hate people who grass. In fact, that is part of the reason I am writing this book: a grass is worse than the Old Bill. But on this occasion I managed to scarper in my car before they arrived.

Things were going well as I met new staff and sent them where they wanted to go. Then the bombshell hit. The Stockwood bird announced that she was up the duff with my baby! My head was rocking. It was not that I didn't want kids, it was just the fact that it was not the right time. And besides that the girl had four kids already. Then there was the fact that the family was nuts! Ok, probably not as nuts as I was, but still pretty much off their heads.

We took a trip to Birmingham, to an abortion clinic. Unfortunately, the new bloke she was seeing turned up and we ended up going toe to toe in the car park. The next day I had another gypsy's warning from a friend of a friend – it turned out that I was lucky to be here as her new man had apparently been up for stabbing me to death. Like the man said who rang me, all's fair in love and war.

A few days later I had to meet a good scaffolding pal from Southmead in the local pub. He had two brothers who were as nuts as he was. We met up but before long all hell broke out and my mate got glassed. The next day I got a call from a local man asking me who my mate was, then he was ringing wanting to know who was asking, but like I said before I am not a grass. How it goes is that when the two men reach each other there will be only one of them standing at the end of it. One will use a blade and the other just his hands and head. Personally, I always back hands and head over people who use blades. On that day I would have bet on my mate winning.

Business in Gloucester was going well and the girls had some pretty weird punters too. Some apparently even wanted to bring their wives along – it all happens in Gloucester! I reminded myself that this was the same place that had spawned Fred West.

The landlord of 26 Midland Road (Gloucester) was beginning to smell a rat – me! I was never quite sure if he used the place or not. Anyway I decided that I better be prepared. There was a place up for grabs in Bristol so I arranged to meet up with the owner of that property and the landlord of Midland Road because he had the cash to put into it. The place in Bristol was a hell hole, really bad; how any girl could work in that I would never know – really it was just an in and out place for a quick wank or blow job. I decided to give it a miss and to this day it's the same. I think they have at least put windows in now – when we first looked at it there were very few windows. I wouldn't have been happy leaving a dog there, let alone having girls working there.

Things went fine for a while until I borrowed the lorry from the scrap man I was friendly with.

I picked up some scrap metal, lots of it, but then I broke down – there was no oil and in that case you are going to end up with an engine going up in smoke. I rang a pick-up man and he turned up out to be a deranged lunatic. Then there was the question of who was going to pay for it – the scrap man or me. Well I was not going to pay for it, but the pick-up man wanted his money and he decided to keep the lorry until he got it. Now I don't do Old Bill – for one reason I've a rope full of hookers on the books. They got that name from Victorian days

when they slept standing up leaning on a rope in workhouses.
Hookers don't sleep a lot. Anyway I had to do something about
the pick-up without involving the Old Bill. I realised that this
idiot was dangerously out of control – he actually put his
girlfriend's name in the death column of the newspaper – but
more about that later.

We left the lorry there in the end. A few weeks went
by and I didn't hear anything about the lorry, although I must
say that the phone kept ringing – I just never picked it up!

One morning there was a knock on the door at the
Vicarage. It was early and I opened the door to the sight of an
8-inch knife held in the hand of a sweet looking bird. Well,
sweet apart from the fact that she was holding a blade! Behind
her was a tall guy but who looked like a real divvy and I realised
that this was all about the lorry. The next thing I was been
bundled into a car boot, although I did not need much
persuasion with a 7-inch bread knife at my throat. Lo and
behold, when I was let out, there was breakfast on the table
with a cup of tea for me! We eventually got things sorted out.

I had got into the habit of using the Luckwell pub every
week. A lady called Lynn had the keys to the door and she was
single but had two lads from a local nutter that was a bit off-
putting. She had not been separated from her old man that
long but we moved in together and I was getting involved and
even serving in the bar. One night when we were out at a party

we bumped into her ex and he looked at me as though he would like to kill me. He didn't do anything so I just ignored him. The next thing he was coming into the pub and grabbing a steak knife, shouting that he was going to kill me. He had his arms around my neck and the steak knife in his hands. I was shouting "Do it then! Do it!" Well I am still here to tell the tale so you will guess he backed off!

Lynn's pub was falling apart and once again I had to borrow a lorry to move things around. I was still running the hookers so everything was pretty full on. It was back to my old friend the scrap man. When I got back to his place he went green and looked like he was about to shit himself. The load on the lorry was enormous – I've always had the knack of loading the impossible onto lorries. Off I went to get rid of the lorry load. Next thing I was tipped off that the barrels had to be moved again; they could not go back on the lorry. Luckily I knew the owner, who tipped me off that security were on my tail, so therefore I got rid of the lorry load – scattering it all across Bristol.

There was a knock on the door and outside were the Old Bill and a security man saying I am under arrest! We all walked around the corner but, what do you know, there was nothing to be seen! The result was that I now had two death threats that involved me being put in Chew Magna lakes with concrete boots on, or alternatively me having my throat cut.

Chapter 6 - The Vicarage, The Gloucester Flat and Connie

Out of the blue a girl stole my heart. She was 'bang on' looks wise and a party girl too. No man can stop himself falling in love when Cupid's arrow strikes. In the end I don't believe it will even matter what the girl does, and in this case because she was a lady of the night the sex was out of this world! She introduced me to one of her mates, and she was as happy with a girl as a man. Sex is stimulating so have a look at your partner and if she isn't fucking your brains out, have another good look – because life is short. Now Connie was the girl who stole my heart but that was a long time ago and now I am afraid that my heart is more like a swinging brick – or so I am told!

Connie was working at the Vicarage and at the house in Gloucester at 26 Midland Road, and her sex drive was unreal. I was getting pretty fed up with the whole scene at that time, especially with some of the married men I knew who used The Vicarage. They were safe because I would never grass; I really didn't mind what they did for kicks, although I cannot stand the thought of youngsters being used by those evil perverts who prey on kids – so all you kiddy fiddlers out there make sure you never bump into me. I would have them all handed over to the kid's parents to give them what they deserve. The courts are weak when it comes to paedophiles as they can get less time than a robber! There must be a reason for it and I reckon it might be because a few lawyers and judges are into that sort of thing, so they go easy on them.

Eventually Connie and I went our separate ways and I was gutted really, I think she was too, really. Lucy was still running the top flat but I had my sister wanting to know what was going on in The Vicarage – be fair sis, we all went to church on Sundays! You have to remember that I will try to turn a penny into a pound.

It's no wonder that the whorehouses are so busy – married men doing to the girls what the wife at home wouldn't do. I had always wondered why hookers and whores do what they do and now I knew. Drugs is one thing and their childhood experience is another, fathers and even brothers touching them up and worse as they were growing up. I don't know of any hooker who does not have an issue of some sort. I have known mothers with daughters on the game – their own kids taken into care when they have been touched or hurt which is the lowest of the low. I will not name these people because of the kids, but I do wonder at a mother who can damage her kids.

At the whorehouse at 26 Midland Road in Gloucester we faced a bit of an unusual problem. Next door they started digging up bodies – turned out that Fred West had been our neighbour at 25 Midland Road! Apparently, he had first started killing there. The first I knew of it all was when I was coming back from a party and found the Old Bill next door with big white tents up. Not exactly good for business! We needed to move on. I think the Old Bill were on to us anyway as they were always popping in asking lots of things about who ran the show, although admittedly ours was not as big as the one next door!

We left it for a while but the Old Bill were everywhere so the girl that was running it fucked off with the takings and anything that wasn't screwed down. Some time ago the house at 25 Midland Road was in *The Sun* newspaper apparently being used as a whorehouse! Well, in my experience, Gloucester is a little fucked up – the men are anyway, certainly the ones that used to come back time and again to 26 Midland Road. And I learned that the Old Bill there were as corrupt as anything too – in fact that was in the papers too, but I knew long before that story broke! As long as I can take the piss out of them I will do; remember I hate them with passion.

I was still operating from The Vicarage and doing very well on holy ground, especially once the man that rented downstairs moved out. However, my sister had given me a move out date – just after I put new kitchen in. We took that with us but we didn't do a very good job with the plumbing and we flooded out the downstairs. I am sorry sis but you know I am a born survivor!

So now with both of my properties gone, I was just bumming around job to job. While I was in jail for another stretch for fighting, I got a letter telling me that I've got this bird pregnant. Well not much you can do in jail about that. It did come back to haunt me though! I was working for myself and for anyone prepared to pay top dollar. I was in a cafe by a school when who should come along but the bird I got pregnant – telling me to do one. I was eating dinner and not in the mood for a stroll down memory lane. She was shouting the odds about the child I had with her, but hey – it takes two to tango, right?

Some years passed with me losing lots and stealing anything that could be stolen. I was getting pissed and moving around. I came across an old mate, Peter the cleaner. He was a good man and we set up in a place up in Hengrove. It was to cost around 5 to 6 thousand to sort out. It was a 3-bedroom flat above a fish shop next door to the Throat Cutters pub. It was a good place but I think that all the violence in there deterred a lot of punters. We had a slow start but we had a lot of new staff from up north. Girls would come from all over UK – hookers, like scaffolders, will travel for work so no one knows what he or she is up to – what's that old saying? *What happens on tour stays on tour!* So the place was earning enough for a sandwich and a packet of chips a week! It was not a great outlet and finally we packed up and left.

Sex is sold in every country we can think of, as well as the old sluts that give it away. Thinking should be changed because a man can fuck anything female and be seen as a Casanova but when a woman does it she is an old whore and a slut – seems a bit unfair to me. We are all the same aren't we? Men and women both love to have sex, good or bad. 70% of women fake it, we are told; I wonder how many men would be that interested if there was nothing at the end of it? Men need to know how to treat women – make them feel loved and have the pleasure of knowing she is satisfied. I love a woman that knows what she wants in a man.

A woman needs to be shown a good time too – not just used. Make sure you find that little sailor in the boat. Believe me, I've come across women that don't even know how to find it themselves – not their G spot, the man in the boat. You know what I mean, play with that little thing. But be gentle with a lady and it will all be wonderful.

I've had lots of threesomes and they are great too. Women only though! I was back horsing around scaffolding – it's not getting the work in that game that is the problem, it's getting paid! I was back on DESIGN SCAFFOLDING now and it really doesn't matter where you are in UK; if you want a scaffolding job then go for these boys – a major firm still working as hard as ever. This is a firm you can rely on and the owner has always been a good friend. They work from South West Bristol but they are a major player in the whole of the UK.

I was living with my friend John's mother – she used to take in the jailbirds or waifs and strays – what a woman! My work clothes would be washed and back on my bed every morning. She was like a second mother to me for a while.

* * *

I was working hard again now, and I had met someone who ran a massage studio in Bristol for the main players. It was all about to happen – this young lady who was a little mad or maybe lonely was seeing a friend of mine, another Paul. He rang me and said: "You need to meet this girl."

So off I went to meet them at a party in her parents' house on a sunny Saturday afternoon. I took a good-looking girl with me, Max, in a nice Mercedes I had put my name on. It was a good party – the sun was shining and there were lots of lovely people there too. The girl my mate wanted to meet was drunk, on her hands and knees. She had fallen and hit her head and there was blood all over her face... but she seemed like a nice girl. I never mind a lady having a drink but I really cannot stand women who are falling over drunk. Whoever you are girls, a lady or just a lady of the night, it is definitely *not* a good look. Drunken women in my experience can be a lot worse than drunken men. Anyway I left the party and gave her my number, after getting drunk myself.

A few days later, I got a call from her asking me to meet up for a drink. Why not? I thought. Little did I know what the results of this meeting were going to be. Madness! We met up on a Friday after I finished work. For some reason we ended up going to the worst that Bristol had to offer in the way of pubs, from one shithole to another. We ended up in Hartcliffe. I had to get back home and she was very drunk so I asked her to get a taxi. But not her. She just got back in her Fiat Panda and crashed into a parked car down the road! The next day I found out that she had been arrested and eventually got a one-year ban.

Now for someone who had made the effort to get away from hookers and trafficking and all that went with that sort of life, I couldn't help feeling that I was about to get on a hell of a rollercoaster ride. Something was telling me to stay away but I was now 35 years old and not ready to give in yet, I was still up for a challenge. I love a challenge – and I was about to learn a lesson about love and war!

I did not hear anything more about my mate's girl for a while but then out of the blue she rang me – so off I went for a second date. Now, don't get me wrong; I couldn't forget that she ran a whore house for the main player and should probably have 'groomers' tattooed on her forehead, including my mate.

It is not a nice game to be in and I had got out of it once, but they seemed determined to drag me back in.

On one Friday afternoon I had been at the dentist having teeth pulled out and not feeling my best. But I met with her and her mate New Zealand Sam – a lovely looker, but also a whore. It always baffles me; why do they do it? I suppose it's a means to an end. We had a few drinks, then met up with a bloke who turned out to be carrying a grudge against me about a van we used at work; I had told him he could not have it to walk his dogs. I needed to give putting food on the table priority before any dog walking. But he was really pissed off and decided to go complaining to the girls rather than me. Now I am not shy of having a bit of a scrap, but I told him to shut his mouth and he shouted back that I should get the hookers out of his pub, as if it was his name above the door.

"Mind your own business, bastard!" I shouted back.

He came running towards me and launched himself over the table.

I am old school, trust me; if you want to hurt me I am going out my way not to fucking let you. He came back for more so I beat him again outside the pub to shut him up. I made sure that the girls were OK. The Old Bill were on their way and I got an ambulance for him.

In the meantime I had picked up two men who were after me, so decided to make a move. Who should follow me but my date! She was drunk and ran across the road without looking. A van hit her hard and she flew up in the air, landing 100 feet down the road. The ambulance arrived for the bloke I had beaten up but I pulled it over for her. She was taken to hospital and I wanted to head there too. Meanwhile the bastard I had beaten up is whining to the Old Bill that I have glassed him.

"Well, don't be so nosey in future," I shouted back at him.

I can use my hands as well as anything else that comes to mind.

So now I've got New Zealand Sam telling me to come on and really I just want to shut this bastard up again, but the Old Bill were everywhere. A copper was asking me what had gone on so I told him I needed to get to the hospital to see my date, not listen to the bastard shouting his gob off. The copper looked at me and then at him and said: "Do one, go on, get out of it."

God bless you my son as you're the only copper I ever had any respect for – although maybe he thought it would be too much paperwork to fill out.

I came back to see my mad woman the next day and she looked like a lorry had run her down. This had actually been our third date. On the second I had crashed the firm's van outside another pub the week before, with her in it, and we had to get away from there pretty sharpish too. On our toes you could say. She decided to get up out of bed and leave the hospital – now this is one tough cookie. I took her into town to get a new top as she was still wearing the gown from the hospital!

I had met up with this city boy, well man really; he was from the local city crew where I grew up beside Bristol city's ground. He is a good bloke, not many about these days. At the same time, Amanda and me moved into a flat. I discovered that she had done well for herself – flat paid for, kid on the way – I never hung around putting out kids!

I was back working and she was running a whorehouse masquerading as a massage parlour. Any massage studio is a whorehouse or a house of ill repute, in my experience. Strangely the law seems to overlook this, and I wonder why that is. I think it keeps the rape down and lets all those perverts get their hand on young girls fresh to the game. The Government should sort it out. The Vice Squad trawl around but all they do is visit places looking for underage girls or people who shouldn't be there.

Chapter 7 - Taking Care of Business

Now that I had another daughter, called Rose, I was looking for a house. I was also thinking that now might be a good time to go straight. My other half could do her own thing, but I wanted to close down the brothel I had set up in Avonmouth with an old flame, Jackie. The camera and video had disappeared and no rent had been paid so I went over to see what was going on. What I found was a very angry landlord threatening to put me in the meat mixer – the type of thing that should really only happen in films. I had 12 hours to find the rent in order to keep my fingers and toes. As the whorehouse was above a burger maker – specialising in horse no doubt – I didn't fancy the chances for my fingers and fucking toes if I didn't come up with the money!

I was getting to a point where I could trust no one, not even the bitches I had been fucking years ago – cheers Jackie; oh, and Tracy. Anyway the money was paid.

It was time to put something else together and I was thinking of a courier service. I eventually came up with the name 'Stork Couriers' because I wanted to get it based on a charity CLIC in Bristol that help children and young people with cancer. I thought this might be a good way for me to put things right a bit. Anyway I put my idea to the cry-baby Mr Wiggle, his name always made me laugh. I met him when he was working on the same scaffolding firm as I was and one day he just broke down crying over a woman.

"I know mate, it's tough but stop fucking crying – it's been two days now and you haven't got out the lorry!" I said.

Well Mr Wiggle thought about my business plan and liked it so we went for it – Stork Couriers! We put a lot of work into the signage and the writing on the van was out this world – a stork with glasses carrying a baby in a net with a feather in the baby's hand. It had the CLIC logo on it as well.

It was very hard to find work as we had to keep working on the scaffolding and we struggled on for a bit and then I decided that I needed to do something else as well.

I came across an old yard in the middle of city centre and now I really was turning every penny into a pound! Mr Wiggle was not up for it; it was too rich for him so I went for it alone – 8000sq ft. of parking space. So I had an office for the courier service and the car park was going very well. It was on Charles Street by the new courts they were building. From there I started to hire out cars – old bangers, with tax, MOT and insurance – but I soon realised that the cars attracted parking tickets and speeding fines and of course the shit who had hired the car would be long gone before those tickets dropped onto my mat. Another lesson learnt for me: no fucker is going to want to pay any ticket if the car is not theirs. I had started to meet up with lots of people including one called Andy from the King Charles pub – what a man!

The car park was going from strength to strength and a man called Paul Sparks was running it for me, parking and cleaning. It was bringing in about 80 to 90k a year in cash! When I took the place on no one told me who to pay rent so for about 3 years I paid none! Lots of nurses from the BRI hospital used the place – it was just up the road.

Now Stork was taking a beating, but I just picked up a bike for it. Little did I know it was a bent knockoff. A couple of weeks went by and I put the motorbike away down at a mate's house. There was a knock on the door to the flat and it was a crybaby wanting his bike back. I had had a hard day on the tools and I did feel a little sorry for the bloke. It turned out that he lived up the road in Henbury. Anyway I said I would try and get his bike back to him. I knew all about the Old Bill popping around to the flat a few days back looking for a bike – about 5k's worth they reckoned. I gave the bloke £250 and I thought the job was done but he rang me crying again so I said I would drop it round to him. My mate wanted his money back but I could not stand the crying so I went back to the Lamplighters pub.

When I arrived at the pub, it was not my mate waiting but the CID. At Stork Couriers our logo was 'the caring couriers' and this prick had gone to the Old Bill. So now I am up in court for fencing stolen goods. The judge was some fat fart nodding off at the bench – perhaps he had a hard night in a whorehouse somewhere the night before, but the case got put back for reports as he wanted to give me seven years! I thought he must be on drugs or had a hard spanking the night before in a little house of horrors. After the report I had 240 hours community service and a £500 fine.

CLIC got to know that I had been caught with the bike and dealing drugs so that was the end of my short spell of going straight! We lost the courier company and old Mr Wiggle was not too happy.

* * *

The car park was in good hands – lots of parking tickets and all that. My partner had a little girl called Savannah and she brought tears to my eyes just like Portia did. I am a thinker – a van with no parcel in it – let's sort out how we can do drug-running; no relentless labour like with the scaffolding firms. An old warlord was doing a small job with us – he was an old time drug dealer that had over £850 in a van once and he never even locked it up. What a feeling, not to give a fuck! Well, when they got to count it – about 40k was fake – not the drugs I believe, just the money. In those days it was easy to get rid of tonnes of drugs brought in via horse boxes – oh, and the registration number of the van was something like 999. That old warlord got throat cancer not long back and 10k was posted through his door from a charity. God bless you Paul warlord, it always makes me smile when I think of the times that we had together – if anyone has those plates from that old van I would like to buy them.

* * *

I was walking tall, the car park was bringing in lots of life forms (the good, the bad and the butt-ugly). For three years I had put up with Mr Wiggle of Portbury but eventually, despite everything, we got to the point where we were turning over 1.4 million pounds each year. I always did say that we were not charging enough but no – he knew best. As far as the courier business was going, we were facing a stiff challenge from the bigger boys like DHL and from other big national outfits. I realised that it was time to get out while the going was good and we had not lost too much.

In the car park lots was going on – money, drugs, hookers, even late night shoplifters. You name it, we had it. Wiggle's brother was due out soon from the Marines and he wanted to know if his brother could get a piece of the action. I said yes, but I was going to cut and run. I've seen some things in my life but this twat was on the phone telling a firm in Brighton that had screwed us over on a scaffolding contract that he was going to throw battery acid in their faces if they did not pay up. Well, best of luck with that boys! I was out of there.

I was knocking around with a planner from Bristol Council who looked like Uncle Fester from the Adams' family. My new partner in crime used to say that his personality was like his job and he was not far wrong. He was a head planner and as long you had a back hander for him (the larger the better) then you would get your planning permission. I did often wonder what we had in common, but to be fair he hung on in there and came through for me.

My bird and me were getting on OK but the booze was taking her down a long road to hell, with me trying to sort her out now that work was pretty well running on its own.

Mr Wiggle had met up with a lady of the night but eventually she told him to stay away. Did he take the hint? Did he fuck. You must understand a thing about working birds: you can't trust any of them. We were still owed lots of money from a Brighton scaffolding firm and Wiggle was on the phone telling them he was going to do them with battery acid again. I couldn't work with him anymore.

In addition, the car park was not far from the old brothel in the city centre, with a sauna that my partner ran for the 'groomers' – a nickname for people who run whorehouses. The life style was really beginning to take its toll on me. When it comes to 'easy come, easy go' I have seen my partner loose 100k plus in takings that would be expected to be paid back. Things were not too clever where she was working and the people she was working for were not the greatest. It would be much better if we got set up with people I knew. But, although things were not good, she was not ready to fly the nest. She was pulled in by the woman owner and her husband – once you have been a hooker or a whore then you will never be able to get rid of the stigma. It becomes who you are. From what I have seen, many 'groomers' could just as easily be put on the 'sex offenders' register as what they do is often really no different at all.

I met up with the boss whom my partner worked for in a pub. She had a massive drink problem too and it must have been her time of the month or something because she looked like she had been shot in the pussy. She was completely wasted. I had started to fall deeply in love with my partner despite all the problems with drink and I adored little Savannah. My partner's boss left the pub with a man just by asking if he wanted to fuck her. I thought she might have to take a shower first but off he went with her to the house of ill repute. I did not see her for a while after that.

We were able to send Savannah to a private school on the Downs in Bristol – not far away from the house. We had around 4k a week coming in, me with the labour and car park – plus all sorts of things were still going on down there – I sometimes wonder where all the money went. True I have been knocked for hundreds of thousands of pounds but I have also made several millions.

In whorehouses the landlords traditionally stay very much in the background so that if there is any trouble with the Old Bill they can slink off. That does not stop them charging top rent, however, and it can be a very good way of money laundering. I think that now Bristol whorehouses are mostly run by Dirty Dean from Wales, who seems to have got a stronghold. Not many people are opening up new places but I suppose that it's not the Wild West, is it?

I started to think about the battery acid threats to the people who owed us money. I actually had a female friend, someone I had known for a long time, and her son had battery acid thrown in his face. I wanted nothing to do with it.

Now the old saying of everything being fair in love and war is probably true to a certain extent but drugs are a whole other world. Where drugs are concerned, there are no laws – at least none that are not made up by the dealers. And it can get pretty hairy when they get the hump.

The car park was still going very well but at the same time my partner was starting to go downhill fast as she started to hit the bottle harder. Like most people you read about, I spent a lot of time trying to pick up the pieces. But with the police at the door most weekends it was getting ridiculous. I counted up that in one year I spent 28 weekends in the local nick but was never charged!

Chapter 8 – Conners and Con-men

Now I've started my life over again God knows how many times and for a lot of it to the constant backdrop of my scaffolding business ('Relentless Labour'). I have been let down by a business partner whose methodology was making threats of throwing battery acid in the faces of non-payers.

The mother of my daughter needed another job as her boss kept on moving the goalposts. In the end she asked me to find someone else to go into business with, something I should easily have been able to do myself. But just at that time funds were a bit low so I made arrangements to go and see an old cousin in the scaffolding game. The long and the short of it was that they found an old pub in the area just down the road from my partner's place, from where she had been running the club she had worked in for years.

The sort of people who went to this place were the likes of Charles the spanker and 'glass eye John', who was into very young borderline legal girls. Then there was condom Martin – now this man had a death wish or something weird going on. He would ring up and book to come in but he was only interested in doing that if there were lots of used condoms in the place – the more the better. He has not been around for a while, and I often wonder if AIDS might be the answer – whatever the reason, he disappeared. There are a lot of fucked up people out there and a lot of what I have seen has made me feel sick, but I've been around the trade for so long that I am pretty much immune. And, the way I look at it, everyone needs a good friend or two. Shane ('The Evening Post') is one, but don't tell him anything – or, even worse, show him – because if you do it's like putting it in the local paper. In Bristol it's the Evening Post (hence Shane's name), where all our own local adverts are published, and if they know what they are publishing for us they just turn a blind eye. Money talks, as they say!

At this time the car park was up for sale at 260k – the aim being to raise the money to put in a planning application on it and then put it up for resale. Not as easy as all that, but then these things never are. I mentioned before that the car park site had been on a ten years lease, during which time I had not paid a penny in rent. I was not told who to pay, so for the 3 years I had held the lease it had made 70-80k a year, which meant there was some money around... but not enough.

I went to my Planning Office pal to sort something out. Despite being a big city, Bristol is also a small place and everyone knows everyone else's business there. Car dealers, builders, scaffolders, you name it – if something is going on, then people will know about it.

I had fallen out with the father-in-law over who was fitting the kitchen in the new house. I didn't like to be rude but I had seen his handy work in his own place so I wanted to save the new place from that! We sat down and soon fell out and off he went in a huff and with him the funding that he had promised.

It was now just a matter of finding 100k from somewhere. Who should pop up, but an old roofing boy I had worked with who had a few pounds. I was so stressed out with it all and I thought it would calm me down to have a drink on it back to back. Another good point was that the planner was a good friend of his. I could not help wondering how that worked since the old roofer was a buyer in planning terms. But it confirmed what I had known for many years: business is bent, whatever part of it you are in.

The planner was knocking around with the car dealers and maybe they had things in common too – the prostitution trade customarily goes with the car trade. Once I went to meet up and see a few car dealers. When I got there they were all watching child porn and, in my book, anyone who is into anything like that needs shooting. Even the planner was there, supposedly an upstanding officer for Bristol city planning.

It is a sad, sad world sometimes.

Around this time, I ended up in the Bristol Royal Infirmary with pains in my chest. My old partner took me in and

Sticks and Stones

I was there for 7 days. I thought I had a heart attack, but the hospital said I had not. So it is true: only the good die young. I was only 39 then and there will be more to come on how stress affected me later.

The continual loss of money that I had suffered over the years was beginning to take its toll. I had wound up Relentless Labour. The money that we should have been paid was huge, but the trouble is always getting that money paid to you. When we wound it up we were owed about 300k with an annual turnover of 1.3 million. If you looked at the money we paid out to earn that amount then you are looking around 450k. So now the major player in the firm, Mr Wiggles, wanted to run on it by himself – best of luck my friend. My only advice to you is lay off the frightener tactics.

Despite his moaning, I still say that the van I took from the firm was mine. It was the one I wrote off as I was learning trap and pony in dog trap lane. It got smashed on my way home when I was with an old friend Rich – I admit that it is probably not the best place to take a line of coke, on the dash board! We ended up upside down and I had to call a friend to get us out. I mentioned that Bristol is a small place relatively speaking, and sure enough before I even got home Mr Wiggles knew that I had smashed the van up. Remember I never drop people in the shit – but Mr Wiggles went ahead and cancelled the insurance.

Now that Relentless Labour had gone I had also walked away from the car park. I had met some good people, but also some pretty bad ones. Once, when I was in London with the Relentless crew, I frequently visited a small wine bar and got on really well with the landlady. It was me, Jimme and 'mad dog'. We came and went from London during that time, but we always ended up in the wine bar. Talking to the landlady, it turned out that the place had been an old knocking shop – or so the word on the street went – and the landlady told us that the underworld had owned it. Who was I to say otherwise?

Well me, Jimmy and mad dog continued to enjoy going to that wine bar just around the corner from a pub called 'The Bristol' and eventually we were asked back to a party in the wine bar – or knocking shop. We went and what seemed like the whole of the underworld was there! We met a lot of people – mad Frank was there with a stunning lady. I was joking with mad dog – he didn't know who mad Frank was. Mad Frank was also known as the tooth puller, who used to work with the Kray twins.

I got talking to this man and I take my hat off to the boy: he has done what he has done in life, and he has done what was necessary. We spoke about Cambridge Road and Horfield nick where he and I had both been. I came to the conclusion that Frank was a top man, who reminded me of old boxer trainer Fred Randle. He was from London too. There I was in a wine bar (former knocking shop) with mad Frank and mad dog – how fucking mad was that?

Now in my time I have met many different people – from murderers to rapists to grasses. I had met Jaz and VJ, lads selling coke like it was candy in a candy shop. I was on that trip for a while but I am very glad I got off the boat in time. These guys are Indians and they were supposed to be good friends. They were about to learn the lesson that you cannot trust anyone as Jaz turned 'QE' (Queen's evidence) and royally fucked his friends. He had even stayed under my roof, the dog. Being a grass is always the pits.

I remember the brothers from the Alex club in Clifton who took some gear off me many years ago. Well the story was that they were lifted at the airport coming or going with a small stash. Now that should have been ok – it should have gone to court and been dealt with but the Old Bill popped into the house. No one was in, but they found cocaine all over the place – kilos of the stuff, so I heard. If there is a lesson to be learnt it is not to leave your gear around the kitchen table! Bristol is full of magpies – let's be fair, it was the home of captain Blackbeard some years ago!

* * *

Now I had Mr Wiggles calling me in a rage over what I'd left at Relentless Labour for him and his brother. He was issuing threats as usual, wanting to cut my partner's face off for some reason. I thought that it was way past time that this idiot learned that there are no friends in business. How he ran things after I left him was no concern of mine. There was lots of money owed, and I knew that I was not going to see a penny of anything that came in. At this moment in time, I think he is happy enough running a scaffolding company from Portishead with his brother.

Now I've grown a lot of weed over the years. There was a particularly good fish and chip shop in the Fishponds area that sold a lot of fish and chips, not to mention plenty of weed! These were the boys who taught me the ropes on growing marijuana.

At first I used to grow a bit of it in my own home and then I thought I would give it a go on a more commercial basis and ended up working with some Pakistanis. Now my own experience leads me to tell you never to let a Pakistani into your house telling you that it will be fine to grow some weed and then set you up with the plants and promise to 'look after you.' They will rip you off. So now, as well as me putting up with my partner and our deteriorating relationship, I am putting up with the Pakistanis. I had a whole forest of weed growing and my partner coming home from the pub every day of the week for years pissed – it was like she was ill with it.

I was beginning to reach the end of my tether. It was ironic that we had got rid of my partner's old boss, another drunken cow, but I still had to put up with the police coming around too often about her behaviour while I had 40 plants in the roof of the house. They came around once about a dog up the tree outside – not a cat, a fucking dog! They found one lot of plants and I only got a verbal warning as it was judged to be for personal use. I was smoking a lot of grass apparently, if 40 plants were for personal use!

After this incident, I stopped the growing, meaning we were now living on the earnings of my partner. Her father had backed out of the deal we had had so it was back to my partner's money, and she had earned a great deal of money by hook or crook. I was still picking her up from lots of shitholes in Bristol and this was beginning to wear very thin now. But with the car park gone we needed to have some money coming in. The Pakistanis had first met me in the car park so I decided that I better get growing again. I think my daughter was around 4 then and even this little girl was helping me – I just told her she was watering tomato plants! It was high time to expand the crop.

My little girl was in a school near the house. We had taken her out of the private school and she was meeting new friends. Well, kids are kids and she only made friends with the local Old Bill's daughter! Now I don't like the Old Bill at all but for my daughter's sake I decided that I would be friendly. I had to laugh, him and me sitting at my solid oak table chatting, while I was getting high with a small jungle in the attic of the house! I swear he never had any idea of what was going on. We sat in my garden while I was growing weed and he still had no clue. He was having a beer or two and he would have remained ignorant if my partner had not called the local Old Bill. We had had another rough up over her being drunk as a lord. Eventually we both left the house and by the time they came around there was no one home. They decided that they had better break in to make sure everything was OK and got in through the kitchen. I had another 30 plants under cultivations with the Pakistanis and these were found so I was in trouble again.

My partner's drinking was killing her – three bottles a day with a few shots before work – I could not imagine the effect it was having on her. I was beginning to wonder if I was the one that drove the women I knew to drink? We knew how to party as well.

My partner had asked her mate around lots of times. On this one occasion I remember sitting at the kitchen table and listening to the dog lapping up his water. Well, that was what I thought it was. But no, it was actually my daughter's pet Staffie called Louis with his snout in the pants of my partner's friend who was having her pussy licked. She was someone who worked for the MOD in Bristol. I went mental at first – the dog has never been the same. Sometime later she was in the house again for Savannah's birthday when I caught her again on the bed with Louis, and this time she had to go.

I went to the vet to make sure the dog was ok. My partner's friend clearly needed help. I could tell a few stories about some of the girls on the game – one in particular comes to mind, but more of that later.

My partner was now with the AA. A lot of men from AA use whorehouses and this is how it works. They go to a meeting now and again, then spill their guts. Now you're not telling me that you would not tell the wife or husband when you get home, of course you are! Each person can have a sponsor. My partner had a sponsor so she was making an effort. But in the meantime I was getting sick of doing everything in the house, and I mean everything. When someone has a drink problem, drink is all they think of. The partner and me were head to head again about what we needed to do and then she ended up falling off the wagon again.

Portia's 13th birthday party had arrived and a friend helped pay for a disco while my ex did the food. We had the do in the rugby club and I was looking forward to a good night. The party started about 7.30 with lots of kids, young kids as well. I got chatting with my ex and then out of nowhere came a sidewinder from my ex partner's bloke and there was an almighty crunch to the side of my head! His father started to get involved. My so-called mate took a few bites out of him and the party went right up in the air! Sorry kids – the CS gas was meant for the men but unfortunately the kids got it too. Horrific I know, and although most people were there in good spirit, others were not. If I remember correctly it was at Barton Hill rugby club. My own mother and father had left before it went up and I can even remember I said sorry to my ex's old man in the toilet – I have no idea what for!

Chapter 9 - Drink and Demons

Alcoholics Anonymous is, in my opinion, something like a cult. Once they get hold of someone, it is like they have taken them over. I like a drink myself and at times I have probably overindulged but I just think if people have a problem with drink they need to just give it up!

A bloke called Steve was running AA in the Bristol area and was always running his mouth off about Combat 18, a neo-Nazi terrorist organisation associated with the Blood and Honour organisation. It originated in England but has since spread to other countries. Members of Combat 18 have been suspected in numerous deaths of immigrants, non-whites, and other C18 members.

My partner had lost the business Elite Retreat because she was drunk all the time. She moved around to a shop at the Old Market site to open up with the president. He was married and had a few quid but didn't want to part with any of it. Truth is he used my partner to the hilt, although to be fair he did get things going and spent thousands on the place but he was not as smart as he thought he was and the planners shut him down. On another topic, how the fuck he got away with 9 counts of battery on his bird I will never know. Anyway the planners put an end to my partner's dream and I suppose that the moral of this particular tale is that you just cannot open a place anywhere you fancy, even if you do think you are bomb proof!

One day I was sitting with the old warlord Paul when I got a call about the house from my partner, who was shouting that I should get the fuck out and that it was not in my name. When we bought this house I was not on the paperwork, as we did not want to jeopardise it with the precarious nature of the business I was in at that time. What I didn't own could not be taken in payment and all that. But at the same time I had sunk my heart and soul into the place, not to mention a lot of money, and now it was going to be all hers! So the sledgehammer went with me as I went round and put all the windows through. If I could have got hold of a JCB I would have pulled it down. My reasoning was that we were a partnership and if I was not going to be able to live in the house then neither was she. She was on the drink again with 'the wounded' – her old boss.

I was extremely hacked off for being taken for a mug again; I vowed that it would never happen again. Added to this I had the Pakistanis saying that they were going car boot me – but I was ready for them; I had a lot of anger to get out, and they would do nicely!

I consider myself to be quite a decent man in most things but there is one thing I just cannot get over and that is my hatred for the Old Bill – who, amongst other things, seem unable to protect us. As I am writing this book the news is all about drummer Ian Rigby who was hacked to death by some low life Moslem extremists.

I have a lot of friends that doubt our government in the way they have just opened up the gates to anyone. We can't even provide homes for our own people in this country let alone for any other fucker. I have to say that I have never voted in maybe twenty years. Politicians seem all out for what they could get for themselves and everything is pretty much strangled in red tape. No jobs, no ability to get people off benefits and back to work. In my opinion, if the jobs were made available by limiting immigration then there would be no excuse for British people not to work.

It is difficult to have respect for a country where the bankers are screwing everybody and politicians are fiddling their expense accounts. It looks like the message is 'every man for himself'. We need to bring some pride back to Britain: you can't change history, but we need to put some serious thought into what the future of this country is going to be.

Evening Post rang me after a weekend of partying with hookers and we ended up paying in weed as we run out of paper money. I can remember partying with one or two of my partner's crew - one or two willing hookers, lovely! While the cat's away getting bladdered the mouse will play.

The partner and I had made up, but she had no job again and the 80k that had been spent on the place had gone out the window and they wanted it back as well as the rent. Anyway I had a good night with the Evening Post, what a bloke. I decided to stay at his as I had had a few beers. The next morning I got up and went home. Now I've seen lots of strange things in my time, but as I walked into the house I got the shock of my life. My partner was in bed, covered in blood - I thought she been shot! The door to the house was open and I thought that the Pakistani had been in and killed her. It turned out that she had been pissed as usual and had cut herself smashing the Jamie Oliver plates that I had bought not that long before. I do remember when I bought them they were advertised as being unbreakable – so I was surely due for a refund.

Why had she done it? Because she thought I was upstairs with another woman. I wasn't even in the bloody house!

* * *

On my 40th birthday the bailiffs were knocking on the door. By this time there were around 50 plants in the loft again and here they were to move us out! I had a big sword in my doorway so I stood ground: I was not moving as I knew that the mortgage had been paid. I rang the partner and she was on the piss again. How much more of this behaviour can I tolerate, I am asking my self! Anyway the Old Bill were on their way again. I was off with the dog, Louie, another real party animal, God bless him. Like I said, he had not been the same since he had been forced to lick pussy three times by a woman who clearly needed reporting. The sight of that still haunts me to this day. The Old Bill was in the house for about 3 days doing what they do - looking at my daughter's laptop with Micky Mouse on it, fucking fools.

As I write this book I can't help wondering what has gone wrong with my life. But even with all the disasters I have to smile, because I have been in the dark and out a few times. I wonder if it is time to change, but then again it is being the hard case that I am that makes me ready for anything that life has to throw at me.

-

Paul Scrase

Portia Faye, Paul's daughter

Savannah, Paul's daughter

Mike and Valerie Scrase, Paul's parents

Paul, in his 40s

Cannabis Plants

Chapter 10 - A daughter's perspective: My dad, my friend?

My dad has been lots of things in his life and has done lots of things, some of which I'm sure he isn't proud of. But he always prides himself on two things he got right: my sister and me! Says he "must a done summat right, ay?"

From a very early age I knew there was something different about my dad, compared to other people's I mean! My dad was always the one everyone wanted to be seen with. It soon became apparent, when I hit my teens, that a few of my friends even thought he was good looking too! Something that, I'm pleased to say, never went any further!

I don't have many memories from my early years if I'm honest. This was when my dad was at an all time height of his naughty behaviour I think. I do remember being about 4 and waking up to little letters left beside my bed.... telling me how much he loved me. Him and my mum had a rocky marriage and split eventually for good around the time that I was 5.

I do remember one evening, after they had separated, my dad picking me up from school in his scaffolding lorry. I was 7, maybe 8, and didn't see any harm in this. My mum and grandparents on the other hand were far from amused! My mum had put a restraining order in place against my dad that meant he wasn't allowed to see me unless the visit was supervised. My dad being my dad, however, didn't stick to the rules! We had the police helicopter out looking for us that evening. My dad eventually did give me back, leading to his arrest shortly afterwards.

I had started secondary school by the time I witnessed his second arrest. Aged 11, and "seeing" a Year 9, it wasn't cool when my dad rocked up threatening to hang my boyfriend from the pagoda in my mum's garden! And the poor lad, he was only 13. In my dad's defence he was only acting on the fact someone had answered my mobile and told him "to do one" – which, when my dad is alcohol fuelled, isn't the best thing to say to him!

The neighbours must have seen and heard all the goings on and rang the police. My dad was actually arrested for drink driving after refusing to calm down. This resulted in a ban (one of 8, maybe 9 bans - is that right dad?).

My mother re-married not long after this incident to a man who, as much as my dad hates to admit it, has been good to me. I was almost 12 then. Little did I know that my new stepfather and my dad were about to start something ugly. My 13th birthday party was a right mess... thanks to the pair of them!

It was the party to end all parties: no budget, no rules, no exceptions. Everyone in the school was invited. The hall was packed with drunken 13-18 year olds without a care in the world, till all hell broke loose. My dad, his business partner and my mum's new husband and his father all started fighting. The party ended up being CS gassed. Definitely a party that won't be forgotten! I'm dreading my wedding! Not long after, In August 2000 my baby sister arrived. What a shock to the system! I had been the apple to my dad's eye for 14 years.

An only child, and quite a spoilt one at that, I remember my grandparents taking me to hospital to meet my new baby sister. What could I say? A baby, a bald one too - she won't like me saying this but she was bald until she was about 4 I think. Savannah's mother asked me if I wanted "a cuddle." And the answer was "NO!" Most definitely not, why would I? I left the hospital sulking and carried on sulking for days. But on my next visit to see Savannah something strange happened and I was overcome with a love for this baby that was so strong I knew that while I had anything to do with it, no one would ever be able to hurt her. And even now I feel that. With almost 13 years between Savannah and I, I am a lot older and wiser now and I know every trick in the book. Believe me I have used a fair few of them myself, in my time. But Savannah knows I am always here if she needs me.

I can remember me bribing dad into taking me to have my belly button pierced when Savannah was born. It worked, I don't know why, but it did. We spent the whole day driving round to piercing shops in a taxi, but no one would pierce me because of my age. However where there is a will, there is a way (so my dad says) he made a few phone calls and the piercing was booked.

There is no doubt that my dad was 'cool' - he was the dad everyone wanted. It might have had something to do with the fact that he allowed my friends to swear, smoke or drink before they were officially allowed to - or the fact that whatever he got me, if a friend happened to be with us he would buy the same for them too. I remember going Christmas shopping with dad and his bankcard once, and he said: "Treat your mate too." Now when you're 13 or 14 that is definitely "cool."

Another time, I called a friend on a Saturday night and she seemed very evasive on the phone so I asked what was up. She said: "me and Ross (her boyfriend at the time) are sat with your dad having a beer!" I couldn't make up my mind whether I was jealous or pissed off that I hadn't been invited.

My dad didn't really ever introduce any of his women to me but I do remember one: a police officer! However, the next lady in his life, properly after my mum, was lovely - she would so do anything for me and vice versa. However, it was common knowledge what my dad's "girlfriend" did for a living, something I knew wasn't cool. (All concerned tried to keep it from me, but it didn't take long for me to work it out). I don't think I knew the extent to which the world of hookers and corruption can mess with someone's head. The money may be good, and the lifestyle may suit some, but it's not what it seems. People get hurt. Lives get ruined and I will make sure it's not part of the life of any of my family, ever.

Some years passed, Savannah was growing up quickly. We spent a lot of time together in her early years; I would often go over for the weekend and stay with them in Henbury, Bristol. I never knew what my weekends would consist of, sometimes dad would have cars that needed cleaning, or envelopes that needed stuffing – I always earned my money even if it was a bit more than most people would get for pocket money.

The one thing my dad always taught me is that money had to be earned. No matter what my dad might have done over the years, he is a hard worker and a good scaffolder. At this point in his life money wasn't really an object: his scaffolding business was doing well, his car parking enterprise was doing well. He told me, in all seriousness, that I had to get a job. Get a job? I was 13! But, looking back, I can't thank my dad enough for that. He had got me a little Saturday job in a salon in Clifton village - a haunt my dad liked on a Saturday evening. That Sjob set me up for life. I now run my own salon. Thanks Dad.

From the age of 13 or 14 I spent more time with my dad than I had in years, he wasn't about much when I was younger. Those years were precious. Dad seemed to have matured a bit with age, or so it seemed! I'm sure some would beg to differ.

I have learned a lot from my dad - he may not of been the most practical dad but he has taught me a few of life's lessons! I met a lot of the people that he has mentioned in this book, some of which I didn't like at all- especially uncle Fester of Bristol City Council, I knew he wasn't normal. I saw him a few years ago in a pub, with a friend of mine, who also has little children. He was soon warned!

When I hit 17 and learned to drive, I started to see a lot more of my dad and my sister. This was the beginning of our friendship really. We've had ups and downs -I'm not going to lie, sometimes I've hated him, and sometimes he has made me really sad, but I've always loved him. Now I could drive to my dad's alone - I didn't have to rely on my mum or step dad to take me. I started going over on weeknights and weekends, staying for a week here, a week there. Dad was doing really well. Business was good, his relationship was good, and he had his 2 girls. It's funny how one-month you can be on top the world and within a matter of days or weeks it can all be turned upside down. Things don't always go to plan! Dad's partner was an alcoholic and it was taking over family life. It's definitely an illness - it should never be ignored.

A few years passed with dad juggling business and a pretty rocky home life (not that he was an angel either) my baby sister was being affected by the way things were - she was about 6 maybe 7 at this point. I'm sure she has seen things that no one should ever see, things I'm sure she won't forget. I know I have. The family home was repossessed. Without his knowledge dad's partner wasn't paying anything - the mortgage, the bills, nothing. She always managed finances and took charge, so maybe dad should have seen she was struggling. But she always seemed as though she was on top of the world (even when she was at her worst.) She fooled everyone. It was a huge shock to everyone when on my dad's birthday the house was taken away. I always wonder if it was what she secretly wanted.

The saying "it will get worse before it gets better" springs to mind. They were allowed to enter the house with the bailiffs to gather a few belongings. What can you do, how much can you grab, with men watching up over you? They moved in with the in laws.

Dad had not always seen eye to eye with his father in law (technically they weren't married, but for the sake of telling a tale, it's easier) so this was an experiment to say the least and one that didn't last long.

I think Savannah was only about 6 or 7. There was no hope of getting the house back. So now a plan of action was needed, I'm sure the events that happened over the next years were far from ordinary. Dad didn't stay with the in-laws for long. I think he went on to stay with Nan, then the odd night with me.

His next move was to get his own place in Bedminster (a place I think he felt at home) so he fixed it up till it was looking lovely. It had two bedrooms and I stayed occasionally, so did Savannah.

At around the same time my dad tried to introduce me to Rosie - another 'sister'!

I don't think so. I stay firm to my word. People can't be introduced into someone's life past a certain age and expect everything to be ok - like a fairy tale! I have one sister and one sister only - Savannah! Harsh but I won't change my stand.

However, the new flat didn't last long. The flat was soiled - turned into a whorehouse - to which the neighbours protested, and soon they were evicted! I don't know what it is about that life, it follows people about. But I'm pleased to say my dad isn't into that shit anymore!

From there on it's a little vague. Dad and me had a temporary fall out. I think we had a few too many wines together and disagreed about something! That lasted about 8/9 months I think. It was Nan who sorted it out for us. If it had been left to me and my dad we probably wouldn't have spoken - we were both very stubborn.

This was about 5 years ago. Things have changed dramatically since then. I met my partner and we had a baby - making my dad a granddad at 45 - the first boy for him. I think he always secretly wanted a boy of his own (God knows some may yet crawl out of the woodwork).

It's safe to say my dad has been on an adventure... the good, the bad, and the damn right ugly. Broke the law several times, seen hell a few times, and probably hasn't got a place saved in heaven quite yet either. However, he has changed and is making a life for himself on the other side of the world now...

I believe he has just completed some exams to make him a teacher! Yes, this man you have just read about, is now highly qualified. I am sure he has to pinch himself sometimes too. I understand it must be hard from him to be away from his girls but needs must dad - we will always love you!

<u>Chapter 11 – Behind Closed Doors</u>

I was trying hard to keep my head down - still looking after my partner – she was really someone that everyone took for granted. Her name was Amanda and she was a special girl. Everyone has a talent in life and this girl knew how to make money. But that made it easy for people to take advantage of her, even her close friends. She would always have money and it would be drinks all round, anyone who wanted it.   I've seen her downing 4 or more bottles, not worrying about the price and lying to me on the first, then on to the second, then to the top of the neck of the third. It was always a worry; she was the mother of my child for fuck's sake! Don't get me wrong: if you can't beat them sometimes its just as easy to join them. But she was in constant denial, telling herself she was well or better.

Looking back now, I would have stood by her for the rest of my life, but it is really difficult if there is no trust there and drink will do that - it wrecks people and changes them. I would have married her although she was not the marrying type. Now I wonder how the fuck I put up with it for so long, picking up all the shit and baggage of her life. The money she lost had to be paid back.

The funny thing was that her boss was just as fucked up and I've seen the pair of them blow 25k weeks takings or more – these were two women who were no good for each other at all. I don't really know why I stuck it out so long, but I really did love that girl. She was a clever girl too, had all the advantages growing up, and she had me hooked, for longer than I should have been, but that was the power of the woman and my feelings for her. I fooled myself for a long time that trouble just seemed to be attracted to her, but the truth was that it was her that let the shit into her life. The end result was the same though; I was on the endless trail of pubs, picking her up, off the floor sometimes, in one or another of them. And she was not fussy where she drank, I was beginning to think this is coming to a fucking end soon and we all know that everything comes to a end – love, jail, fucking, violence too.

I have heard recently that Amanda has not had a drink for 7 years now. I have not seen her in a few years. When I was with her she had me like putty in her hands but I had to wise up and ship out. The times that I've been pissed on in bed! It's not good, I never was one myself for pissing the bed, so that made it even worse! Amanda was a Gemini and they are definitely two different people in life, like Jeykyll and Hyde. Now you put the earth sign Taurus with Gemini and it's not going to happen! She was all heart - too good for the piss takers around her, I wish her all the best in life! I hope she can stay away from the drink. Amanda gave me my beautiful daughter, Savannah. I am never far away if she needs me and I love her millions.

* * *

You could end your days in in the nick if you were older than most and you could die in the nick too if you couldn't handle it. I know someone on a drug charge with possession of a firearm thrown in. He had dealt with most things but he couldn't handle the pain, the hurt and the discomfort.

Prison is a place that breaks people. I can understand that more than those who end their lives over some woman or another - that's just crazy, you have to pick yourself up and get on with your life.

In Horfield prison I got to meet mad Frank while he was there for a short while. In the nick your feelings can get away from you, sometimes you can be on a high and then you have to deal with the low. I've talked with murderers, lifers and also with a black rapist once, in the yard. I remember the treatment that child molesters would get in the nick and I have never forgotten a single day of my time behind bars, from the young offenders to the adult prisons. I remember cleaning cells after men had been taken to the hospital wing after harming themselves with a made up blade.

Sometimes men are not guilty. They spend fucked up years in the block where you are put for fucking someone up in there. Drugs are rife too, passed over on visits or any way possible.

I told the story of the big fucker who was raped himself after he robbed an old lady of her pension - not a great idea. UK jails are fucked up, no more then any jail where it's quite common for people to have their ears bitten off. I will never end up there again where the violence is tucked away behind doors with heads rocking and rolling around the floor or being smashed in by the door. Robbers and thieves teaching the way it is - bank robbers, sorry post office robbers, the two twins I knew from the outside. It becomes a way of life for some who end up in and out of nick for the rest of their fucked up lives.

Life can be unreal on the inside. I've pissed and shat in a potty. As I write this it reminds me of a prison favourite, shit parcels - picking someone's shit up after they have slung it outside of the iron bars! Then there are the drugs being brought in by bent screws - get a screw on your side and you're laughing!

* * *

I was back on the scaffolding, jumping from job to job! One night I had to pick Amanda up from Elite Retreat — she was shit faced as per usual, and there was a nosy cow on reception. The girl on duty is supposed to be watching over the girls while the manager or the madam is away. Typically they will be girls who are not sure if they want to get into the game and are selling their soul or sometimes just like the idea of answering the phone because that will do until they see what money can be earned.

The girl had her partner there, don't really know what for, perhaps he wanted to make sure she didn't nip upstairs to make a few quid! Now this bloke pipes up asking me to stand outside - not a problem. I know that this bloke was the son of the dog lover, I am sure you remember the tale about her escapade with my Louis.

I popped outside and before I knew it three had jumped me and sprayed me with CS gas and nearly beat me to death – I didn't quite wake up in intensive care but I was pretty fucked up. This was happening a bit too often for my liking - having me head booted all over the place. But these boys were yellow bellies or jumped up bullies and couldn't have coped on their own. If I remember rightly, a rep got a few blows to my head in to, with a pool cue.

Now looking after Amanda was getting beyond a joke. I found my way into Pembroke to work on an oil and gas site for a firm called Hertel. They were a very regimented firm and treated men like kids - not for me that one, but it got me away from the on-going problems with Amanda, for a while. I stuck it for 10 months or so - I was on the high road again and going back to the Elite Retreat some weekends, kicking the girls out the room so I could get my head down.

If you want a rest, don't stay in a whorehouse. They are party animals - worse then 40 men on a stag night in Spain; they live their lives for drugs and booze. There was a young girl I remember, batted for the other side - she didn't like the job, but just fucked the men for the money. Now this girl had had a pretty rough life. I've known her for years and she came off the streets as whore. She had a heart of gold and I liked her as a person. Her troubles had started early when her stepfather used to rape her. He was high up in something or other. She told me she had been raped by all sorts - solicitors, nappy wearers - it seems that anything goes behind closed doors. They even love to have a bash on one another sometimes, probably because they get bored and don't mind jumping any way just to fill the time!

I knew that Amanda needed a lot of help. Tom, Dick and Harry took on the Elite then gave it back as the water had been cut off and it was paper towels or wet wipes all round. Then the place burnt down, and we never got to the bottom of it – there were lots of rumours about whores on crack pipes - if you ask me the place was a death trap. After that Amanda got out of it again and she went on a mission - a drinking mission - and now it became a game of hide and seek again. I found her in the airport one day. Shit-faced was not the word. I am not sure where she thought she was going that day. Perhaps she was trying to get to her old boss's house as she lives out that way somewhere. Anyway it was par for the course. Writing this I think about when I first met her, she was always blind drunk even then!

I had been asked to get rid of a motor for the roofer. We had to tow the fucker to a place were I could do the burning. Love it! I dropped the motor, came back to sort it later, and took Louie with me. Being a nosy dog, like all dogs, he's got his head in close, and then, all of a sudden - whoosh – it went up in flames and Louie was running down the street, all his whiskers burnt off!

The next time I went out for a walk he was not keen to come.

My mate and I went down to see the wreckage. After we'd had a look we decided that it needed a second go. This time it really went up in flames.

In the scaffold game you get to meet a lot of different people and I knew a cable puller for BT who would put one mile of copper in and take a 100 miles out. The price for copper is pretty good - a nice little earner that can help you start a scaffolding firm.

My old mate Bart - what a bloke he was! I set him up with some birds one night – three of them for the greedy sod! Problem was he had not realised that he was going to have to put his hand in his pocket. He thought he was just irresistible to women I suppose! Anyway I think it cost him £800 for the hour. Bart man, you're fucking mint!

Old Bart had a halo around his head at the Bristol City ground and not for being a good boy either, just for being a bloke that liked football violence. Bristol are right up for whoever wants to take them on. That is not something I get involved with. I have had a few brawls in pubs, but football violence is organised crime. When Millwall went to the Black Horse Pub they put all the windows through – it wasn't even the right pub. I don't think any City lads had used it for years. The place was just full of cider monkeys and pill poppers.

By this time my partner Amanda was in the mental home. I had known she had problems and I felt that there was something not right in her head. Finally she got nicked for robbery – it was the culmination of her life, well at least the last 20 years of being around the whoring game and the drink she had consumed. She finally lost it. She was saying that she wanted me shot. Well I had been down that road a few times. I'd had enough!

I went one better. You might have heard about men who put their other half's name in the death column? Well I had my memorial for her tattooed on my back.

A woman can drive a man overboard. We used to joke about whom would kill who first! Mental illness runs in her family - her mother had been written off a few times, but then again we all have skeletons in the cupboard. I had a grandfather who tried to kill my loving grandmother. He tried to finish her off while she was in the bath, with a hair dryer. Once it's got you, does it ever leave you?

As a boy or young lad I'd been in lots of shit. I remember way back I came home once from college and went to the Tape & Barrel pub - now there's a blast from the past! I went up to the doorman Wayne, an old name that everyone needed to be worried about. Wayne was the first man to knock a few of my teeth out. Anyway, years passed and he was found buried, somewhere in Bristol, so it's not always true that the bullyboys get away with it.

As a boy I was always into money, and I lived not far from a place called Securicor that held a lot of cash. My parents worked there too, and believe me they are straight as can be. If I needed an insider, it wasn't going to be them! The place had been done a few times before. I did not know that someone had done it over good and proper maybe 12 years before, although it was buttoned up so tight that a fucking rat could not get in there!

Sometimes I wonder where my gift comes from. It's not from my mother or father. I think this book is about a boy growing up and the hope that I have been a good father to my kids. I don't think they would want to change me!

* * *

One night I met up with an old mate from prison in the Elite Retreat Massage parlour, Dave who taught me about jail and how to survive in there. Now he was running dirty heroin. Not a nice drug. I was on the spanners' - hard work, but more or less honest. I sometimes wonder if I had stayed in the game maybe I would have been a lot better off. Anyway I was in Pembroke and someone wanted a little dirty heroin, so I started running it up there as I went back and forth. Like I've said, I was up for anything. For money I'd sell my own arse. Then one day I was pulled in, about ten minutes away from my digs in Pembroke, by armed police. Now these boys you definitely don't want to mess with! Guns are not my thing, especially not when they are pointed at me. So I was nicked in a hired van and, to add to my problems, I was banned from driving at the time. s for who tipped them off, all fingers were pointing and at a man I lived with in digs - a mouthy bastard from Kent!

I didn't want to point the finger until I knew it was him for sure so I put up a £500 reward for anyone who would tell me who had grassed me up. All I wanted was a name. That fucker had cost me a lot, not to mention having the police station copper looking up my arse. This copper just wanted to keep looking even although I had told him I had nothing up there!

I was in court again with a hard-faced magistrate and as I was banned from driving, first it was a £1,500 fine and 9 months on my driver's licence again. I've been up for the driving drunk or banned while driving 8 times. I vowed – no more! If you are a drink driver it will bite you on the arse sooner or later.

In my time I have ploughed vans into motorway signs and I've driven into a pub front. I think the law should be changed so that there is a ban and a tag system, where those habitually being caught drinking and driving can drive only in working hours rather than not at all. If a drunk driver kills someone then I believe in a life for a life. But who is handing out the punishments? These days what exactly does it take to become a magistrate? Not a lot, as far as I can see. You just need to be a do-gooder or maybe some nosy motherfucker who has nothing better to do!

Ask me how many solicitors, magistrates and judges you are likely to find in the local whorehouses. Quite a few, I promise you. So please don't tell me that you are whiter than white. I know that from all walks of life men have one thing in common: sex! It's one of the greatest things on earth. Between two consenting adults, every man dreams of it! As a boy I was at it well before 12. Do men ever forget the first time? I think not.

My first time was when I was 11. She was a lovely girl and my first sexual experience. I will never forget her. But this is not the same as a kid being groomed. I was up for it, literally! I had a boys heart all messed up now by having sex at that age. It was a big revelation for me, learning where to put my cock, even! I will never forget that first teacher. Now she is still with the man she married long way back and I am not surprised he is still with her; wherever she went at that time, she won hearts and souls of people. Today she is still as stunning as she was back then. Sex was a blessing with her and it took my virginity and hers. You never forget the first time and we had those first wonderful experiences together. I've had many teachers from that early time and I don't really want to think about who I've been with.

As I am writing this, a lady who was so wrong in a lot of ways comes to mind! She was very pretty but must have had a life of hell! Let's call her Danny. She had worked the street but had gone on to spend the previous 15 years in one whore house or another. I don't think any woman needs that shit in their lives, but hey, who the fuck am I to say that. I have broken a few hearts in my time! Danny used to work at the Elite Retreat. But she also had a massive drinking problem - another very pretty young lady that had ended up following the wrong road. Her situation was pretty typical of the whole sex industry: the game is full of drugs and drinkers and those who had been abused at home, maybe in their early days. Now the Elite Retreat was the best place by far in Bristol, but every single person who worked there had issues, a lot of them really bad ones.

I think that women get stuck in the rut of the sex industry. I've heard a lot of managers say to the woman: "Darling this is not a dating club, its a fucking brothel, so get your arse up the stairs and then when you get there, work it off." It makes no difference if this was the first time on the game for a very young, barely legal girl. It doesn't matter at all, they are there to sell sex, nothing else, and no one cares what other issues they might have. The whore might have to get it on with a 25 stone man or a 60 year old who might bring his own toys to use on her. She would just have to hope that they had been cleaned in between times - who knows where those toys had been? There is no doubt, girls, it's a dirty job.

Chapter 12 - Families

It's a strange thing that sometimes people who seem very close to you really don't know you at all. And Amanda, although I had a child with her, was one of those people. She never really gave me a chance to be involved in Savannah's life; hell I never even saw either of them!

Anyway, I had kind of put them both to the back of my mind until my old boss called me up and told me that he'd had some woman on the phone asking him how she could get hold of me. I knew who it was. I agreed to meet her, and that was my first mistake.

I am sure you know the expression 'let sleeping dogs lie'? Well, that is exactly what I should have done. Looking back on it, it was just about the worst thing I could have done. But I was curious. I had been warned off her, and she was married to another scaffolder. There were death threats flying around and all sorts, but hey, you know me by now, never like to be told I can't do something.

We arranged to meet outside a cafe opposite her older kids' school. I was not welcome - the mothers were all having a go and telling me to do one, no one gave a toss about how I felt. I was not the type who would go back for seconds when I had already been somewhere. I just couldn't see the point, that was all done and dusted and ancient history. Her bloke saw me as a spunk donor but I can tell you I had a whale of a time with her. Her name was Wendy and she had my child, Rose, who had been brought up by another scaffolder. It was a meeting of lust or sex - on the spot, any time - we met up in a toilet or clubroom. I've never had a chance to put things right but when we did meet up some time later it was just the same, hot, raw sex. She still struggles but she is not with her partner. I believe she will find her man sometime soon when the little fellow learns to let go of her. I have never had the chance to get to know Rose as it has been difficult seeing how she has been brought up by another scaffolder with small man syndrome. She is mine but I don't feel I can push myself into her life until she willing to know me.

There were three girls and two boys in the family, and one of the lads was as bent as a nine bob note. One of the girls was my daughter Rose, so I thought I would take the chance to hang around for a while and try to get to know her a bit better.

I had just shut down a hookers' place in Ashton, close to where she and her mother lived. I've got to say it was a bit hard going - talk about being up your own arse. One of her brothers was full of it and looked like a right mouthy type, but underneath it all I found him to be a quiet boy. In some ways he reminded me of myself when I was younger. I liked him and I used to joke about him with his mother but I am afraid that he is going to see the inside of a few prison doors, that one. The middle daughter and I had some issues but really I was just a man with a lot of love in my heart, although up until that time I think I had never really had the chance to share it.

I had to see it from Rose's point of view. Another man, who she knew as her dad, had brought her up. I was just Paul to her and her mother had always, up till that time, told me to stay away. It was difficult for me to think of being a father to someone that I had never known. I had a lot of love to share and the man that she thought of as her dad was not perfect either, with a gay son and a liking for transvestites. It was a strange time, with me fucking the ex again and hearing stories of her other half being nicked with trannies! When I heard that I laughed so much I nearly choked, especially as word travels fast in Bristol. I couldn't even comfort myself that he had brought my daughter up well because he had let her down too. Her mother was wrong to have done what she did, to keep Rose from me and keep her from knowing the rest of her family, but that is what she did.

It was strange I had always longed to have a wife and kids, well I had the kids but by three different mothers! I was pushing fifty and it was high time that I settled down. Could a leopard change his spots? I don't think so. I have made mistakes, a lot of mistakes, but I've still got a smile on my face and I realise that life is a real learning curve.

I think I will be learning until the day I die. I love kids and one of the things that makes me so sad and angry is the fact that we seem to hear so much more about child abuse nowadays. Well, the offenders should be given over to the parents of the children. I know what I would do!

I had moved on to Lincoln by now and met some nice people there, one of the most memorable of which was Adam the cage fighter. He was one big motherfucker and he showed no mercy at all. Then there was Elvis who was the best scaffolder on earth; watching him was like watching paint dry but he was a good man.

Slayer was the seven-foot doorman at the Club of Warlocks - the bike builder from hell, with more than a story or two to tell. It seems that wherever I go I seem to meet the wrong 'uns - maybe I see something of myself in them, who knows? But in the process I have bounced policemen all over the place - there are bent coppers in every town and city, we are all just human with human weaknesses it seems.

I met Mad Mike in Lincoln, and he was a bloke to shoot first and ask questions later, bless him. It's like I always say: its not what you know, its who you know! One night we were out on the town in Smelly Kelly's and I managed to get my face broken in half by a local boxer. Now I am always up for a challenge but little did I know that the visiting pool team were all gay boxers. I was blind drunk and when I am that out of it I can't see straight. The pub was full of gay hay bailers and farmers who batted for the other side! Another new face was the mad preacher who I remember for the fact that he was drunk seven days a week and blind as a bat.

I suppose that my message to anyone who is in love and happy is never make the mistake of thinking that the grass will be greener elsewhere. Take it from me, it never is. My life has been full of drink, drugs and too much partying. It has fucked me over big time, always chasing an easy buck and falling prey to drug dealers who literally wring the life out of people. There are not many shortcuts I have not tried, but I never have really understood why. Maybe by the time I finish this book I will have a better idea.

We go through life meeting people we like and dislike. If you are someone that I don't like, you will know all about it. I am generally very distrustful of people and I never tell anyone anything I don't want to be made public. I know that they will be singing like a canary if the price or the inducement is right, or just 'cos they can't resist it. They end up telling their granny, who tells the person next door, and then before you know it every fucker knows. There are maybe two or three men in my life that I have trusted and even then it was a sort of cautious trust. It is sad, but sometimes those people who reckon they are your friends are really your worst enemy. They can stab you in the back and take your trust and throw it back in your face. If you don't watch them they will be screwing your missus while they are slapping you on the back and smiling!

It was different in my folks' day, as they knew no other way and stayed together through thick and thin, till death do us part and all that. Now I have all but given up on British women; they are too high maintenance for me, at least the ones that I have met. A nice lady from the Ukraine or even the Far East is best I reckon. They know how to treat a man.

* * *

My next venture was to start up a little enterprise and grow some weed - that's me: couldn't help getting up to no good wherever I go! Despite what it might look like I have tried from time to time to stay on the straight and narrow. There is no doubt that my parents taught me right from wrong and in fact I have been the only one in the family who has ever been in any trouble. So do I blame myself or do I blame other people? Well, I know that other people might have had a part to play in leading me astray but I seem to have a major blind spot where it comes to learning from my mistakes, and that has made it one hell of a life. I don't even know what I have been looking for in life. Maybe if I did it would not have been such a struggle! I think I also sort of believe that life is mapped out for you and whatever you do is not going to change the way it goes a lot; pretty much what is supposed to happen, happens.

For my next move I was off to Germany. Well it was not a great move because, apart from not particularly liking Germans, there seemed to be nobody anywhere in that country who knew how to put up scaffolding. I was with my mates and colleagues Steve and Camie and we worked our bollocks off over there. I couldn't help wondering where the famous German efficiency was. Given the lack of skill they had for scaffolding, it was no surprise to me that they lost the war!

All the while, my master plan was to dig the biggest fucking hole and build a big barrier in front of it and just grow weed in poly tunnels and chill. I was ready to set up just around the corner from the Indians who had ripped me off for eighty thousand pounds.

Chapter 13 - Getting a Life Back

I decided that I wanted to take my life back. I was sick of being pushed and pulled this way and that. I have been on an endless quest for love and I have not given up, I know it is out there somewhere for me.

One thing I do know about is scaffolding. I know it inside out and upside down. I have worked 24-hour straight shifts and although I know that there are a lot of imposters in the scaffolding game, I am the genuine bonafide article as far as the old spanners are concerned. Scaffolding has taken me all over the place and given me the chance to meet all sorts of different people. And somewhere along the way I have stopped being afraid of dying, although I know I will be fighting till my last breath, whether that is a car boot ride to my destiny or death from natural causes. I know that I have love to give and I started looking for it in the Ukraine. How that will pan out I don't know, but as they say, watch this space! Now from no one to love I had a choice of two lovely girls and I am in torment because I did not want to hurt either of them.

My life might look like a road map to hell. I might look like a hard case putting a brave face on things. But all the time I knew my past had not finished with me; it was going to catch up and put the boot in again. I've got a temper just like the next man but funnily enough nowadays it is not the anger that keeps me awake at night, it is the thought of love!

I have grown into things like jazz music and horror films that would scare other people rigid. I have regretted with bitter sadness the loss of people like Amy Winehouse, a beauty with a voice that no one will ever forget. My life has been a mixture of ups and downs. I was told once that I would travel. I didn't particularly want to, but now my life changed in a big way. I was working in Saudi Arabia so it looked like that prophecy had come true. Who would have thought that scaffolding would bring me to the other side of the world? But then it has taken me to a fair few places.

Many of you will have had scaffolders working at your home at some time or another. If you have and you are easily offended then look away now! I've been on jobs where the guys have made free with the house and paraded around in the lady of the house's pants after going through the knickers drawers. Grown men wearing their work belts parading around in little knickers or tiny thongs. Ladies, check your panties from now on - and the fridge - we will eat you out of house and home. Scaffolders are a breed apart. If we make up our mind to do something, trust me, it will be done. We are weapons of mass destruction if we need to be - just ask any copper, they know. And when we are pissed out of our brains a fuck off warning is needed. The streets that we own are rough. It's a matter of kill or be killed.

I knew the killers were out there, but it has never really made much impact on me. That was until my daughter was walking down one of those streets and had a knife pulled on her. Now as her father I could arm myself with guns or knives or even a fucking baseball bat. I would do life for any of my kids, in a heartbeat. Just remember that I am only ever a plane ride away from my kids, and yours, if you want to take me on. It comes down to a simple rule in life: hurt someone and get hurt yourself. Besides which, blades are for arseholes!

Now it was the simple things in life that I craved. I wanted to find a girl that I can treat like my queen for the rest of my life. The Indians are still hot on my trail but they are fucking fools. I heard that they were stopping scaffold lorries looking for me - as if! I can tell you guys that we scaffolders don't give a fuck and we stick together. Let's put it this way: I would offer you the sole off my shoe. But your head would be under it followed by a bit of jumping up and down on your skull, a little trick old bummer Lewis taught me a long way back. He always said it was not a good idea to leave a bloke on his feet too long, as he might hurt you.

Now the word on the street is that the old Elite Retreat has been turned into a gay house. What the fuck is going on?

Gay men are unheard of except in the gay village in the Old Market where the whore houses are crammed into the back of the run down shitholes there. The world is a funny place.

I always wonder why those ladies of the night would be happy to give up half the money they earn to people like I used to be, but then I suppose the street hookers are often raped and abused and end up with nothing at all. Bristol is riddled with the heartache of ladies going home with pockets of cash while their old man never knows or pretends he doesn't know where it comes from. What she has had to swallow or how many times in the day she had been gagging on some prick! Just appreciate what your women do gents; that money has been hard earned. She's not packing shelves in the supermarket.

Well the world turns and it's another day and I was now in the Middle East. I am not the greatest fan of flying but off I flew from Scotland to the Middle East and left some good mates behind. I worked hard and could earn 14k in ten days in the land of the rag head - in the heat of Saudi, the land of oil and lazy fuckers! I take my hat off to the expats who make this country work. I don't think they would get a drum of oil out of the ground if it were not for the foreign labour that is the backbone of the country. I am here, like most other people, to earn, save and come home and be a bastard again - only joking!

You can earn and save a lot of money in Saudi. I was training scaffolders. It was slow going though because it took about three days to get done what would take three hours to do in the UK. I can't see the time when they can do without expats coming around any time soon.

The hotel they put us up in was no great shakes either, but I knew I would be moving on to a nice compound that the company owned where I would have a lovely room. I met up with people from all walks of life and soon found out that knowing my job and teaching it to students were two very different things, especially in the Middle East. Shopping is a challenge too: you have to say things over and over again before they get it - buying a top up for the mobile phone is a real challenge, they really don't seem to have a fucking clue. I think when the oil is gone the country will be given over to camels again. But then again by that time we will all probably be on horseback in the UK!

Chapter 14 - Sticks and Stones

In good old Saudi I was beginning to look like a chicken! Good God, they eat a lot of chicken in that place. Of course being a Muslim country, and all that, there is no bacon or pork chops on offer, but bloody hell they make up for that with the amount of chicken they eat. And it is not like any chicken that I have every eaten before either. I suppose I was starting to enjoy being there, although it was a long way from home. It was an eye opener and a new life for me and I met new people, some of whom have become friends. The management was OK and I had had a couple of trips to Bahrain that were nice too. This was definitely the best way to earn a crust! There are certainly compensations of being so close to Bahrain. The women there are wall to wall, and there are always drinks on the table. It seems to me that wherever I go in life it is always a journey into the unknown.

But wherever I am there is one common understanding and that is I am very likely to break a face or two, or have mine broken. Yet again, I'm full of mixed feelings. It's a torment, a turmoil of love and hate. I have come to a point in life were I must behave, be true to people. But I was given the name of 'The Bandit' by my oldest sister for no reason. She is a sister that I have a lot of love for. Oh, and there is the little matter of being in a place where much of my old behaviour might cost me my hands or my head, and because I am quite attached to both it meant having to straighten up and fly right... at least for a while.

I was here in the land of the eternal chicken for one reason: to get on top of my life and get rid of my past destructive ways.

My partner Amanda was in the past now, she made her bed and she will have to lie in it. We were happy once but she ruined it and I can't live life like that, it's not for me. I will be coming back to the UK with a woman on my arm, a woman that any man would be proud to have by his side.

There are a lot of reasons to live and to fight on for, as well. I have got the seven deadly sins tattooed on my legs to remind myself that I am capable of doing any one of them, several times over probably! But there are also tattoos that remind me of how lucky I am to have my kids and my lovely Portia and her son, who are my life.

* * *

I have watched the film, 'The Prisoner' that shows what lengths a man would go to find his kids. Someone once said that trouble follows me. I have watched a lot of films in those early days in Saudi. If want to see a film that you will never forget then watch 'The Flowers of War', based on a true story.

Perhaps I have just been at war with myself all my life. That's the thing about being in Saudi - you get plenty of time to think and look back over your past. People are basically the same, whether they are in Saudi or in Bristol, but some of the guys out there had been there for years and putting up with the 4.30am call to prayer that never fails.

I just hoped the people who live here had some respect for the men that keep their country together and the money coming in. I've got to say that it did get under my skin that in Saudi churches are not allowed - while in the UK we bend over backwards to please every fucker. Not that I want to go to church, but it seems a bit off balance that it's not a two-way street.

Let me tell you about the prisons in Saudi, too. They are a long way from your average nick in the UK. No windows, no light, no TV, hell not even any beds! People can be kept underground blindfolded and in general I would say these conditions serve as a pretty good deterrent not to break the rules.

If you are caught doing the business with another man's wife you get your head cut off, although it takes two to witness it. For the light fingered there is a 'three strikes and you're out' policy, and that means lose one of your hands and go to jail. If that does not show you the error of your ways, keep going to offence number six. Then you'll have to hire someone to wipe your arse, 'cos you will lose the other hand. Seventy lashes is a pretty popular punishment too, and that might be the punishment for being seen with someone who is not your wife or if you are caught indulging in gay activity, although I'm not likely to get into trouble on that score.

Chapter 15 - Some Thoughts on Love and Life

You can buy anything in any city if you dig hard enough and if you want it bad enough. You can sell anything too, to people in business or whoever wants it. Money will buy you everything from a hooker to a gun or any other tool of death. Although I love the city of my birth, Bristol, I know it has a dark side... but I can't help loving it just the same.

Trafficking is something that goes on every day. Girls in whore houses are trafficked, and told to just lie down and be quiet when the fat arsed Old Bill pop in and break the door down. The managers back the owners or sell them out for a get out of jail free card. It is a fucked up game where whorehouses, like the best hotels, get star ratings for the quality of their services. The ages and other details of the girls on offer are like a welcome mat rolled out for kiddy-fiddlers. Now, wild horses and all that, but even I have decided that a church door is preferable to the back door into which the low life creep looking for young flesh. The runaways know that and come to the whorehouses offering themselves up and lying about their ages, and managers ask no questions while the paedophiles lick their lips.

Every whorehouse should be checked out for underage girls because I've seen what the man next door can do to the life of a young girl. No father or mother wants their kid to end up being drooled over, and worse by old perverts. If mothers' could see their daughters being preyed on by these monsters surely they would die of grief? Having said that, I have seen a mother and daughter on the same shift. My ex partner is apparently back selling herself in hotels, ducking and diving. It's not a life and all it has done for her is to ruin her health. Yet, when things were very different, she bore me a child who is my life.

I think that at long last I have learned to turn the other cheek. That's not to say I am going to take any crap from anyone. No one fucks with me. I know what I want and what I definitely don't want in life. I've taken my fair share of shit and handed my share out as well.

I met a Russian girl; and hoped that she could find the real me and make a connection. Initially I loved her because of the warmth that even thinking about her brought me. Well, love is a funny old game and I know that my own battles will always be there for me to face. I suppose that you could say that I am old school: hurt me and you'll be hurt too. Well it turns out that she and many, many more are just out to fleece you. I suppose you can't blame them, but it has been a big wake up call for me.

I never really thought I would travel in life; really, people like me usually don't. I've met some fucking loons but I also meet good men. Surprisingly maybe, the scaffolding world is full of possibilities for travel. It often goes hand in hand with a life of crime. Most never get caught. Business turns a blind eye.

I'm no different to any other man, and I think that I can count my real friends on the fingers of one hand. One good friend is Jay, a man who split up from his wife and then went back to her five years later. He had a sister, a good girl, now also settled down with kids. I can't really do the going back thing, once it is over; it's over with me, besides which in a lot of cases there have been one-night stands. I would not have a hope of saying how many over the years. Now though, I'd had enough of all that and I was really looking for a soul mate. And the internet is certainly not short of choice for a guy who is looking, and in every country in the world from China to Russia.

When people talk about the Middle East, there are some really good people here from the USA, UK Expats - the people who keep the place going really. I was there training people in the art of scaffolding and to call my students lazy was an understatement, but hey, I was not here to judge. I'd never liked being judged so I suppose I should not judge others. The Saudi people were all OK and I got on very well with my students. They treat you like a Lord really. But now I had moved on to Bahrain.

With a blade of death on my back, and despite what I have done and look like, I still care for people and have the best of intentions. But then sometimes (well most of the time) luck is a word I don't really use.

My old partner,Amanda had chosen that time to ask me to sort it out with her but I couldn't do that, and her old man would have been far from happy! It will be interesting to see what she ends up with in life. I think I am a good father to my kids -well at least the ones I know of!

I was 48 years old and thinking of starting a scaffold firm in Bahrain. In England you pay too much tax and with the price of petrol, people are hard pushed to run a car or truck. In Bahrain and all the Middle East fuel is cheaper than water! But there is always a price to pay and I missed my family.

Perhaps the Indians I have had dealings with back in the UK should take a leaf out of the books of their countrymen working out here, who manage to live on next to nothing. I worry about foreigners in our country taking advantage of the benefit system, schooling and health services, and I can't help feeling that it is going to get a lot worse. I don't think you can even find a Londoner in London any more.

Drugs are everywhere, in every country of the world. Even in this place, which is supposed to be so strict, I would say that drugs are rife. From what I have seen the Middle East is worse then anywhere else I've been.

As I look back, my mind wanders back to Kelly who nicked the TV that was not even mine. She was a hell of a fuck! I don't know why it is my mind keeps going back there but I do take my hat off to that lady. Kirsten you blow my mind and Donna likewise! Connie - time well spent with her, I hope she has the world at her feet! Kim from school, fuck me she was a naughty girl, Wendy too. There's been so many and all I have ever looked for is just THE one. I have watched my kids being born and in my opinion that is the only thing a man should never miss. To be there as your child arrives and is put where it belongs, in its father's arms that is something that cannot be beat!

In the Middle East boys can't see girls unless they are married, but boys wander around holding hands with each other. It doesn't seem right: my students are holding hands, and I just had to get used to it.

It was not something that I understood at all but hey, desperation can make people do all sorts of weird things. Anyway these good time lads grow up and marry and then they go the other way and they can have 4 wives and God knows how many kids! I heard of one with 30 kids. Bloody Hell it seems a bit fucked up to me, but then each to his own. I can sort of see that someone might hold hands with his brother, or maybe a close cousin, but this lot take it to another level.

I came to work in that shit hole to earn money. It took them 10 weeks to get me here - that was pretty much a disaster as I lost earnings having given up my job up in Scotland. Still, I thought, now I was there, things would improve. But no, then we were left waiting for payment. They still expected you to fly around and pay your fucking way, despite the fact that you had seen no money. I was thinking of taking the fucking mugs to court over my contract. They are a multi-million pound company, English too.

Still at least my life was consistently unpredictable. I still had a smile on my face. I would have just liked to grab the moneyman and put his head in a vice to see how tight his pockets were! One thing after another! They should have sorted out all this before they brought people out to a God forsaken place, because if they have no trainers there is no college. They should also pay people on fucking time. I am a man who will speak his mind, always. I never liked not getting paid, although it seems to be what my life has mostly been all about. When you don't get paid it fucks you up all the way down the line, paying people, paying bills.

Now the city of Bristol has dog fighters, badger baters and dogs in bars just sitting waiting for all sorts of low life scum.

We have become a country with an open door for all kinds of drug pushers', criminals and whores. In Saudi I have seen the results of fanaticism at first hand and I have not been impressed by the way that the men here treat their families. They believe that a suicide bomber will go straight to heaven and be given God knows how many virgins as a reward. What about the virgins? What is their reward? Then Ukraine had massive problems and I wonder where it is all going to end, you might have gathered I have a lot of time for introspection out here!

I really do worry that the planet is being destroyed with one war after another and that we are abusing every single resource in it.

* * *

When it comes to luck I've got none. I flew back to Saudi only to find that my visa had run out. Just had to let the red tape take its time, I couldn't be bothered to worry anymore! It didn't seem like rocket science to sort out a visa that covers the right period, but then hey, we were in Saudi.

I just laugh at it all really but does anyone else have luck like this? I hope not. My time is coming to an end as I've now been on planet Earth longer then I am going to remain on it in the future, so its time to be the man I am, whether I like it or not.

People meet and make friends, but be careful of the people you think of as friends. Family is the best friend you will have in life. There will be lots of ups and downs but you will never find a better friend than your mother and father or sister and brother. Other people never are what you think they are. So from now on my new family will be my only glory in life, the only problem is that I haven't got them yet, but it will happen and I will support and love my new family like the old one.

I've finally become that man I should have been years ago. Mother you are an angel, the best mother ever. Father you will never be forgotten ever in my life. I know what I've put you through and I want to say sorry for that. I have a mother and father who I owe my life to so I send you my love, always!

The word 'relentless' describes me well! I know one thing in life: no fucker will try harder than me…. and I am still trying to this day. I believe there is a girl out there that I can make truly happy. In fact, I still believe in my life. It's just a shame that I have had to get to this age to realise all that I have and all that I really want in my life.

I can leave behind the memories of going from cell to cell, police station to police station, dressed in white, sometimes covered in blood. From being woken in places I should not have been for weeks and weeks and year on year, just lurching from one disaster to another. Life is life and you have to take the rough with the smooth. My criminal record is as long as my body - longer I would say. My name is Paul John Scrase, born in 1965 around 7.30 am just playing the cards that I have been dealt.

Chapter 16 - A Mother's Point of View

I have known Paul since the day he was born and before - I gave birth to him on the 29th April 1965. Paul was a happy and contented baby and he slept well from only a few weeks old. I fed him on demand. He had a will of his own, even then, and always knew what he wanted. He had an older sister who was two years and nine months older than him and they were quite close as children. When the children were little we lived in a nice part of Bristol, known as Ashton Vale. Behind the house there were playing fields with a stream running through the bottom of the garden. I remember Paul and his friends used to fish in the little stream and he would come running back all excited to show me the tiddlers he had caught in his bucket.

As a family we would go on walks across the fields to Hancock's Wood and to Ashton Court. Paul had a great childhood and went to the local junior school that was just around the corner, until he was old enough to go to secondary school. His early school career was interrupted quite often by severe bouts of tonsillitis and at one time it seemed that he was at home every other week.

Eventually he had to go to the Bristol Children's Hospital for a decision on whether or not he should have his tonsils removed. When he was examined they found that he had a hernia behind his belly button and a cyst on his testicle. Over the next few weeks he had his tonsils removed, then his umbilical hernia repaired, and his testicular cyst removed. Paul was not at all happy with having to be in hospital and would not even speak to us when we came to visit. He would just turn his head away from us and sulk!

When Paul was six his younger sister was born and he did not take at all well to that turn of events. I think he felt put out because he was no longer the youngest, the baby of the family. Another issue was that he had wanted a dog and we had told him that he could not have one until his baby sister was a bit older. We eventually got a dog when Paul's younger sister was three, but then discovered that she was allergic to dogs. This meant Cali, as we had called the dog, had to go. Paul loved that dog even although it was not with us very long. I think that the experience made him resentful of his sister and without his father being around very much (he worked very long hours, twelve hours seven days a week) it was just him and we three girls most of the time.

We did have some nice holidays. Paul's dad always took his holidays at half terms and over the summer holidays. We would often go to Blue Waters Holiday Park in Weymouth.

Paul did not get on very well at school, whether it was the early disruption due to his ill health or something else, I don't know. I was soon to find out as the school pulled me in to say that they thought Paul and all of us as a family should be seen by an education psychologist to find out what was at the root of his problems. We did want to get to the bottom of what Paul's problems were, but we had no issues at all with his sisters and we did not want them put thorough a lot of questioning to try to get to find out what was troubling Paul. Looking back now, I do wonder if maybe we did the right thing by Paul, but it was uncharted waters and we really did not know what the problem could be.

I am sad to say that there have been times when I wondered if I had been seduced by the devil on the night that Paul was conceived. I think describing Paul as a Jekyll and Hyde personality would be accurate. He eventually left school and went to college for a year in Bircham Newton in Norfolk where he had been sponsored to study scaffolding. We would go up and visit him some weekends but we noticed that he had changed. When he came home, he was sporting the first of many tattoos. Still, I have to say that he completed his training and started work for the company that had sponsored him. He also learned to drive, although he always wanted a motorbike. Thankfully, he changed his mind when our next-door neighbour's son had a nasty accident and Paul went to visit him in hospital.

Paul had now started going out drinking and getting very drunk. Looking back it was the start of his troubles. I am quite sure that he never realised what he put his dad and me through in those days. For example, one Friday night he went out saying he would not be back late. He was still not back by morning. Saturday passed and there was still no sign of him. Sunday came and there was still no news of him. I remember the awful feeling that overwhelmed me on the Sunday morning as I did some ironing to take my mind off Paul and I heard on the local news that a body had been fished out of the city docks. I felt as though I had been kicked in the stomach. With shaking hands I called the police hardly daring to ask if it was him. When Paul did finally come home, he was amazed at how worried I had been. He said he did not know what all the fuss was about.

Another Friday afternoon Paul came home very much the worse for wear after a drinking session but still turned around and went out again in the evening. We found out later that he had come home in a company truck and parked it around the corner. Despite the fact that he had had a lot to drink, he took the truck out with a girl in tow. He, the truck and the girl ended up in a field upside down. It was a miracle that neither he nor the girl was hurt. His behaviour was out of control and he ended up being sent for an eighteen-week detention at a youth offender centre in Portland, Weymouth. We would visit him when we could. I remember one visit in January that we made, when he still had some time to do. He eventually came home a few days before his twenty-first birthday.

While Paul was away his father bought a lot of scaffolding from the company he worked for and a friend of Paul's helped to strip it all down. The side of our house was full of scaffolding propped up waiting for Paul's return. His father thought that he might straighten up if he could work for himself and the scaffolding was his way of offering Paul a fresh chance.

Paul had had many different girlfriends, but I remember one in particular - a really nice girl that he went out with for a long time, who came to visit Paul in Norfolk with us several times when he was doing his training there. I really liked her but over time I noticed another name being spoken more often and realised that Paul had probably found a new interest. He had always said that he would not get married until he was thirty, but by the time he was twenty-two he was married, buying a house and had a baby on the way. Their baby was lovely, a beautiful girl whom they called Portia Faye, but it was not long before Paul's wife wanted to go back to work.

Paul was still in scaffolding and working for another company so I was on grandma duty. I would pick up Portia Faye and drop her mum off at work. Then it would be back home for the baby and me or out to visit my mum and aunt. They were happy days spent with a lovely little baby. I used to do this babysitting for them two to three times a week. Little Portia

Faye was only ten days old when we had her overnight for the first time. It turned out that was the beginning of a routine that saw the baby staying with us most weekends and holidays until just before she left school. It was a time that I would not have missed for the world, as I am sure there are not many grandparents who get to know their grandchild as well as we were able to do.

Everything seemed fine but there was just one little worry that I had and that was Paul's drinking. I comforted myself that he and his wife mostly went out together, although often they would go out separately and I think that is where their problems started. They did not stay in their house very long before they decided to sell it and buy a flat in Kingswood. Paul also decided at that time that he should go out on his own again. For a while things seemed to be going well, Paul worked hard and played hard. I still worried that he was drinking too much and although he had no qualms about going out alone he really hated his wife doing the same.

However, overall, things seemed to be going well: Paul had taken on a partner and he and his wife had decided that they would prefer to live in a cottage they had seen in Hanham so they let the flat and moved in. It was a very pretty home but there was a problem with damp so they decided that they would not go forward with buying the place. So now with the flat in Kingswood rented out and having given up the cottage in

Hanham, they had nowhere to go. They ended up coming to live with us. Paul's eldest sister was already married by this time and his younger sister had moved out, so there was plenty of room.

It was great to have my granddaughter living with us and Paul's dad could enjoy having her around more too as he was not working so much. Paul was still working with his partner and I was working full time. The downside of having Paul and his family living with us was that I would see things and have to bite my tongue. Overall though, things were going well and Portia Faye was going to nursery at the school that Paul and his sisters had gone to. Looking back now I think there were definitely underlying problems.

Then one day I had a call from my husband while I was at work telling me that Paul's wife was leaving, going back to her flat. She had asked him to let me know when I came home, as she would have gone by that time. I left work immediately but by the time I got home she had gone. She picked Portia Faye up from the nursery but did not tell them that she would not be coming back. To this day I do not know whether or not Paul knew that she was leaving. She had gone back because the 6-month period for the tenants to whom they had let the property had ended, so she could move back in. Paul stayed with us.

Next thing, Paul's partner at work decided that he wanted to go his own way. Paul found a new person that wanted to go into partnership. I met the man and instantly did not like him. I tried to tell Paul that if he went into partnership with the man he would end up losing everything he had worked for. He didn't listen and it gave me no pleasure to see my prophecy come true. Within 6 months Paul was bankrupt.

The flat in Kingswood was lost and a lot of bad things happened at that time, much of which I knew nothing about. One thing I do remember from that time was the fact that Paul had gone around to the flat to see his daughter and found another man there. He went mad, even though he and his wife were not together. His wife called the police and by the time I got there the police were on the scene and in the middle of a stand-off with Paul. That ended in a struggle with two policemen and Paul in the hedge. Eventually they ended up on the ground with one policeman pinned down by Paul and another officer on top of him.

The police wanted to charge Paul with the very serious crime of assaulting a police officer but after I told the solicitor what I had seen, who had been appointed to represent Paul, the police dropped that charge.

Portia Faye still came to us most weekends. I knew that it suited Paul and his wife for me to have her so that they had time to do their own thing, but I loved having her.

Eventually they got divorced, although I was quite sure that Paul still had very strong feelings for her. I think that they had too much too soon and were very young really. It seemed that they could not live together, but they were miserable apart too.

Whatever the ins and outs and ups and downs, their lovely child was a blessing and the best thing to come out of their short marriage. Portia Faye has grown into a lovely grounded young lady and has given Paul a wonderful grandson. His ex married again and, after a lot of soul searching, we did accept the invitation to attend the evening do of their wedding. Her new partner is a lovely man and has been very good to her and to Portia Faye. I have stayed in contact with her over the years and always say that she has been an excellent mother.

Paul then had a string of different women until I began to be aware that there might be someone else special in his life again. That was confirmed when one day in the car park at Aldi, I had bumped into Paul there and he told me that we were going to be grandparents again. I met her not long afterwards and was told a lot of lies about what she did for a living. By this time Paul had already moved in with her.

Chapter 17 - What's it all About?

Now I know you can't plan life and that sometimes, despite your best efforts, you don't have any control. I think I have given up believing in the word lucky although I hear the word used almost every day: you lucky sod, you lucky fucker, but never aimed at me!

In my time I have been to hell and back, and all I have ever really wanted was a girl to look after before this hell takes my life one way or another: mind that bus - the bomber on the street of our English soil - a hijacked aircraft. Our souls, our truth. When I sit and look at what I've done and what I've had over my life, I should be sitting on a beach somewhere, drinking a cool beer.

Maybe you are there in a holiday hotel with the wife - there is a chance that the noise you hear next door is some hooker having her ass banged because I don't know any hotel in the world where there aren't any on call. Remember also that she's having a tidy sum of money slipped into her silk panties, so she is going to make a noise like a cat from hell. Men, remember: a lot of hookers talk after you leave or after they leave you, so try and do your best or they are going to rip the fuck out of you. I think they are like the arse bandits Indians. They like it best when you leave the shop smiling, but they will always have the last laugh at you boys.

Maybe I should have done what the teacher said and behaved better when I was a lad, but I was always standing in the corner. Let's be fair now. I know why I fucking hated school so much and like I said to the teacher, what goes around comes around. She also made me eat fucking rice pudding and I was sick all over the old cow in a dinner break. My mother is one of the best ladies in the world, the pain she suffered through my growing up was no doubt crippling at times, and I regret that. Let me ask you though, some of my mates think that life is mapped for you. I think that kids these days should realise that they can't just do what they want in life as it gets you fucking nowhere at all. Life is a circular map that we live - day in, day out being taught and told what to do. Ask anyone who knows me; just don't tell me what to do! I've bent every rule in the book and I'm still bending them. These boys have seen more money than most but I find not being able to find true and lasting love so hard!

I was on a flight once, talking about dying, fuck knows why. It was some young lad writing to his daughter because he had a brain tumour. He was telling her how life is hard and that we can only live as long as God lets us, or our bodies survive, until it's time to go. Now whoever you are my friend, I say a prayer for you and your daughter as life is short but no father or mother should ever have to do what this poor bloke is doing. My heart goes out to you.

When I look at pictures of my family and kids this is my regret: not really knowing them but still loving them like any true man does. I have just been looking at my youngest child who I love very much. She is a 13-year-old girl that I've bathed, fed and hugged but still it feels as if I don't know her.

The Internet is full of woman blagging money from everywhere and anywhere in the world. I think they would be better off in a whorehouse that the old bill turns a blind eye to. I look at people and watch and listen to men of all sorts and I just think they have not fucking lived. They do this and they've done that. I don't talk about what I've done or what I can do. keep to myself and I hope when I've written this book all the wrongs and rights of my life will be laid out. I have suffered with money - not getting paid, not being able to pay. I have often thought: just throw me a fucking lifeline. You have to keep smiling, pick yourself up and start again. Yes I really am fucking relentless!

I wish I had worked abroad years ago for the good money. I met someone on the net and I played the game - girls please send me money! It's a wicked world out there and listen up scammers, you will end up with no money and no women. I know love is blind, we live it, we need it, we have it all around us, but also men and women fall in and out of love like hippos in water having sex.

I knew I would find the girl of my dreams and that she would not be English. Now though, I had seen Chinese girls and they were a special kind of girl in Bahrain.

Do I have regrets? Well, sometimes I wish I had gone another way in life. Maybe the right way, but then maybe I was not capable of doing things the right way, maybe I just had to go through the shit in my life. You will never be able to change what you've done but I do need to change what I do in life from now on.

I carried on having money problems with the firm I worked for - chasing money, wages never on time, chase, chase! I would think: what is it all about when a multi-million pound company can't get it fucking right? I would get so wound up that I want to re-arrange people's teeth - telling me it's been paid when it so had not! It's a shame really as people just kept leaving, I guess they got fed up with it, but you are only as good as the trainers here and having a manager telling me its been paid then spending money chasing your money - teeth should have been going missing. When a man does his work - pay the man!

When drugs are involved there are no laws and now I have changed my ways. I've met good people - Old Bill, managers and trainers - but I know that I am the only person that can change my life, no bounty hunter or fucking Indian will do that. I can't stand the kind of life where I am looking over my shoulder all the time. I seem to find peace once in a while and then the horrors and the shit hit me again.

In Bahrain the phrase wall to wall pussy comes to mind. I was there sorting out the hire on a truck and as per usual, it took a while - 3 days to be precise. So I popped in to see this Chinese woman - hard to guess her age, anywhere between 20 to 40 plus, like lots of them, working her soul off for kids and sending home money. They are persistent. As soon as they see you, they are on you. I met many of the girls. It opened my eyes to the pain I may have caused in life, being the way I was. The place was really dingy with low lights – that might have something to do with camouflaging the ugly ones. I watched while they were knocked back time and again till a bloke who was blind drunk walked in. He was easy pickings.

The place reminded me of the old Dug Out Club in Bristol - not a lot of people would know that, it was a long time ago - it was the same sort of shit. I am not sure that these girls are here for the money; I think they are looking for a way out too, a better life, a rich man maybe. Men prepared to marry whores or hookers are always a chance for them and what they are hoping for. But for me they are no different from any hooker in the world; they are all looking for a way out.

I will say for the women in Bahrain that they are smart and know how to treat a man. I am a people watcher, watching them watch their prey. Bahrain has hundreds of hookers all

looking for the road out, maybe not out of Bahrain but out the game of selling their souls. Some are looking for that man just to love them like no other man has. I think that women sell their souls without paying in some way or another maybe all their lives. Every hooker and whore could write a book with the story of a fucked up life.

The food is also very good in the Middle East but they will try to take the piss out of your pockets. I think Bahrain is different from the rest the world, one of the oldest truths in life - you like, you pay... in one way or another. So please gents don't get one up the duff - whatever you do!

When I think back to the days when I was in prison, I often think of the many men in jail and I just don't get it. I tried so hard not to end up there but I am still not sure about what awaits in the future. I know that there is a part of me like other reoffenders that just does not give a fuck. Jail is like every thing else in the world - it will always be there and is not for the faint hearted as it breaks many men. I think that an offender will always re-offend as its always going to be part of their life. I think it just stays with you in your mind running around in your head and in a bizarre way, knowing that jail is always going to be there if you need a way out. For a rapist or child molester I think only hanging is good enough, or to meet the family you have fucked up or the small child that will remember the things you have done to them, forever. There are all sorts of people who will fuck up other people's lives time and time again, whilst getting away with it!

* * *

I am now renewing all my tattoos - no pain, no gain! Laws are to be broken in any part of the world and so the Muslim 'no tattoo' bullshit is as well. Body decoration is as old as time, world wide. When I look at my life I think, fuck me where has it gone? I reckon I have some ground to make up in my treatment of the fairer sex!

I am used to the back street life and it seems to be part of all cities and towns, all over the world. I think I could find trouble anywhere. Although I have been doing my job 33 years I had to be trained. I didn't mind being trained, but I wished it could be by someone who knew the job not by some Scottish idiot telling me to do what I could do in my sleep! I just felt like filling his head right in. I must be changing, though, because I just thought fuck the prick, I'll rise above it.

So now I thought that this side of my life had changed 80%. I needed a girl in to make it 100%. It's about other people now rather just myself, not that I've been a selfish fucker as I am far from that, but I do wonder what is going on.

I was back in Saudi and good or bad, so be it. I had spoken to a good friend called Bart. I can count on the fingers of one hand the real friends I have but Bart is genuine and he makes me laugh.

When your life has been knocked off centre so many times you start to fight back by knocking other people. Now, though, I don't give a fuck what the other man is doing or the bloke next door or the ex-wife. I was young and reckless; maybe I could have a re-run?

This book is about me - if you are here it's because sometime in life you have been fucked with. Now, though, I don't care anymore. My life is going to change and I am going to look for new ways to keep myself amused that doesn't land me in shit!

Long ago I used to set fire to anything I could and break in anywhere I could and do anything I shouldn't. I do have regrets about never being right in the head.

I want now to make my life work so here goes.

I'm the son of a true mother and father that I could never replace. They've gone through it all with me. From car theft to breaking in and out of factories to setting fires – it has taken its toll on my face. I've met men who don't think twice about taking a life, whilst running hookers. I am not scared to tell the truth about the pain I've seen, the pain I've never wanted to see or cause. From GBH to ABH - stamping on heads to being stood on; growing weed, and paying hookers in weed on a three-day bender.   But behind it all is a mind that never stopped thinking of how to live peacefully with my loving kids. I would have liked to teach them or any one who reads this that crime does not pay.

Before time runs out I will sort myself out: no drugs, no hookers in any shape or form. The girl in my life will be here soon and, as I said, someone I will give my life and soul to and maybe a little boy or another little girl. I want to leave riches to my kids. I am a family man, perhaps not quite right in the head, but my life will not be complete until I find that angel I can marry! A good man needs that angel instead of the grief I have caused and suffered.

Now I sit here with a lot of time to myself but I wish I was with the kids, even if not with the mothers.

I just want that little house with a big garden.

Have you heard the saying: 'boys will always be boys' or is it men will always be boys? I've dumped loads of asbestos on the local drug dealer's front door, or should I say back garden. This drug dealer has the largest feet I have ever seen and has spent more time in prison than he ever wanted. Like all good family businesses his son took over and is also doing time. I was locked up with the prisoner who knocked his door one night and bound and gagged the size 13 feet. No one in Bristol can keep anything at home as there's always someone willing to take what you make. I am an international trainer in what I know, but still willing to open my door to any friend or foe. I hope you take care reading this book and learn something from my life story of being a boy and a man with regrets.

'Could have done better' was what was always written on my school reports. I suppose nothing really changes. There are things I am very proud of and my children are on the top of that list, but I could have made it easier for myself, that's for sure.

Chapter 18 – All Mixed Up

Sadly I find I am still mixed up in internet lies. The only good thing is that I met someone who knows a thing about lies and has a life more fucked up than mine! I'll call her Sammy, a girl from Thailand who needs help. Sammy has been worked and she has been abused – she has been to hell and back. She is 36 and a good-looking girl and she really has been through it. She has carried a child that she did not want, and I felt that I must do something to help her. One thing I do know is that it can be rough for a Thai girl in the Middle East where they are seen as little more than a commodity.

The way Sammy had been treated was almost like slavery or trafficking. She has had her passport taken from her and I thought that maybe I should try and buy the passport back for her. Risky I know, but I just felt I had to do something. I knew that I could be getting in way over my head but I just could not sit back.

It is not un-common that your passport is taken off you if you work in the Middle East. This is usually done because your employer needs to apply for your visa. This document allows you to come and go and has to be applied for by your employer. There are many young woman - and I mean very young women - being trafficked. It is really a kind of slavery and they just work in return for being fed and housed. he same monotony every day.

In my madness I felt I needed to put this right but do I buy the passport or just run over the lady doing the trafficking? I am not sure really but I know I have to help Sammy. I may be in above my head here, but we will see. I've met lots of people out here all taking back handers at work and fucking about out on their wives. I've also met Bill. He is from Plymouth and has been working a long time, maybe about 25 years in Saudi alone, and he reminds me of my old man - he is ex navy too. I wonder sometimes if I should have joined up but then again I just don't like being told what to do!

I was working teaching the managers here. But they are far from what you or I would recognise as a manager - they have no people skills, no skills at all really, one is from the underland not underworld - the land down under! However, to be fair he might have people in the underworld since we sent our entire criminal element there in days gone past!

On the brighter side, through Bill I met some nice people, husbands and wives, and strangely enough it turned out that one lady used to run an escort agency. Well I have seen it all, so no problem for me. All the while though, whatever I was doing, I had thoughts of Sammy running around in my head. I had a text from her asking me to help and I agreed. All I knew is that this little lady has the dirtiest laugh I know and a smile to die for and is about 5 ft. 3 inches. And I had to help her.

I was looking to start up a firm in scaffolding as there is definitely a gap in the market for it. Another bloke I met was called Jimmy - a good man who played the manager for a fool. How he ever got through I will never know because a scaffolder he definitely ain't. And then there is Duffy the ex bus driver, well all I can say about that is if you can't do it then you definitely can't teach it.

Bahrain is a playground for the Saudis. Through the week they live like monks not doing any of the things that they want to and then come Thursday they are all over the bridge and pouring into Bahrain to fuck about and get pissed as farts. I found it hard to get used to men wearing dresses, it would not suit me but then again it might be quite cool! For them Bahrain is their own private Disney World and boy do they hit those rides hard.

I know I have not been a saint in my life but I have a big heart. Believe it or not I am really a one-man, one-woman guy - I just have not found the right woman yet. Now time is passing and if I want to have some of the tranquillity and peace that a solid relationship brings, I need to get on with it. I just want a girl with a heart as big as my own, not one who thinks a lot of herself or who is only with me to bleed me dry. I don't want to be a man who needs to sneak in the back door of the whore house because he is not getting it at home and has no way of communicating with his wife.

I suppose I am looking for that old favourite: a wife who is a whore in the bedroom and a wife at all other times! And talking about lovely women there are some real stunners here amongst the Arab women in Bahrain, lovely beautiful women who would take a lot of beating for their looks.

Back to my quest to help Sammy. I had come around to thinking that the best way to help would be to buy her passport and then see her on her way home. Anymore than that was probably not going to be possible. I think it is true, the world over, that a beautiful woman can be a man's downfall! I am aware that helping Sammy does not come without risk and that risks tend to have dire consequences here in the Middle East.

I often think that it is a good thing that we do not know what is ahead of us in life. I have certainly plumbed the depths of life, been a cokehead and a pisshead and have walked the walk of shame on many a morning. I was certainly not born with a silver spoon up my arse and I know a victim when I see one. Little Sammy needed to sort out her life and decide what she wanted. I decided that I would buy her passport but only if I knew that she had got it clear in her mind what she wanted to do. I felt like I had to do this; don't ask me why, I just had to.

Maybe it was a sort of payback for all the shit I had inflicted on others in my life. There had not even been any sex, because I thought she needed to rest, to give her self some distance from the shit she had been in receipt of, where people like her are bought and sold like watermelons. I didn't know much about her but I knew that I had to stop the cycle that she was in, the gang rapes and the other abuse she had suffered. A lot went on there that a blind eye was turned to, sadly.

I felt weak at the knees sometimes when I saw Sammy but I knew I had to keep my head and get her out of this. The poor little thing might just as well have had a chain around her neck like a dog, and abused as well. I don't know why she in particular hit a chord with me, as there are many more like her, God knows. She melted my heart and if anyone tells you that men don't cry, then it's rubbish.

In prison I have seen men cry like babies over the smallest thing. This will be the last trip down that kind of blind alley for me, after this I am going to devote my attention to making the most of what I can be – or will I? Watch this space!

While I was making my plans for Sammy, didn't they go and move her, chain and all? So now if I wanted to help her I had to find her first! In the meantime, true to form, I met someone new called Linda. I met her while I was pissed and there she was the next morning, in my bed, smiling up at me.

I was surprised at how the situation in Bahrain wasn't that different to anywhere else - whorehouses, gay boys and backhanders. The training school that I worked for was full of bullshitters, like the manager who had no skill at all except for sacking people and pissing them off. And while it was difficult for people like me it is damn impossible for people like Sammy who have no way to complain and no one willing to help them.

I know right from wrong, although I have done wrong more than enough times. But I am good at my job and I have come to the decision that there will be no more English girls for me. The girl with the chain caught my relentless heart, but other than that the world turns and I was up against it again with another employer who loved to get the work done but was not so keen to pay for it.

My life has been lived well and it has been rough at times and I reckon I should have a good few years' left in me. In the time left I really want to turn things around but how can I resist the lure of the gain and what I have to do to get it?

From growing weed in lofts and even brazenly in the garden, being one step away from sleeping on the streets, taking drugs and having my collar felt on many occasions - I have been there and back. If I had all the money that has been owed to me over the years then I would be a multi-millionaire by now. It is bad enough being owed money but then if you owe it to other people it gets really difficult. I was so tired of chasing what is owed to me. I worked for one of the biggest training companies in the world and it was still an uphill struggle to get anything out of them and to understand why they appointed managers who were completely useless. And the company went through staff like a chicken laying eggs. I don't even want to think about how much money they owe me or how much they have cost me with their chaotic ways. It is all I can do a lot of the time to stop myself hitting someone! And that might still happen.

In some ways it was like living in the Wild West, a rough and difficult life where you have to live on your wits and the only rules there tend to be written in blood.

Chapter 19 – And so on

After all my efforts with Sammy, she is now back on the doorstep and wanted a second chance. I suppose that everyone deserves that in his or her life but how many chances do you give? I come from a country that is supposed to be civilised and it is completely fucked up - so what hope is there anywhere else?

I told Sammy that I would be a friend to her, and my heart was yet again on another rollercoaster ride. Sure we all have past, she had hers and I had mine, but did I really want to become her lover? Well I was not entirely alone in the decision as my landlord - who is a banker or a wanker (I never could tell the difference) - was kicking off because of hookers being around here. He was happy enough for me to cook meals and all sorts but came over all pious when he saw Sammy!

You have to realise that hotels there cater for all sorts, for Muslim gay men and anyone else who is getting a bit on the side that they should not be. And what harm was I doing with a hooker? None! He needed to wind his neck in or I might just do it for him. Perhaps he would like me to drop a word in his wife's ear? I always say live and let live!

Back to Sammy and her second chance. Now you will understand my dilemma when I tell you that this girl was stunning. Sure she had been almost worked to death by others and I know that she would not have chosen this life if she had any choice, but she had none.

Now I was no stranger to the life of prostitution and all that goes with it, as you will know, but I have to say the hooker scene her in the Middle East is like nothing you have ever seen before. There is a steady stream of men coming over the bridge from Saudi to enjoy an evening with the ladies of the night here in Bahrain and then scuttling off back home before the wife wakes up in the morning.

I am not saying that every hooker in these parts was a raving beauty. Some were as ugly as sin - but Sammy, now she really was lovely. Where exactly she fit in my life I don't really know, and I know that beauty is not everything, but with her in my life it was hard to keep remembering all that and even my judgement of her was influenced by how much I enjoyed being with her.

They say that beauty is in the eye of the beholder but Sammy would be a beauty in the eye or any beholder, believe me. Standing having a shower with that lovely lady, I knew that she was always going to be very special to me. I have tried to get away, far from her, but her sweet smile that is hard to resist. I loved the colour of her skin and the sweet words she used to tell me, how she fell in love with me. It is true that everyone needs a chance in life, and there is no doubt that when I was with her I was always beaming from ear to ear.

Life was beginning to change for me. I really and truly do not care at all what anyone thinks of me, and why should I? Don't forget I have been rubbing shoulders with the lowest of the low and I know just how vile people can be.

I think from my experience that many hookers are like crackheads they need something to pay for their habit although in their cases it is not so much that they want drugs, although often they do, it is more to do with keeping their kids from starving and having no other way to support them.

When I look at this book I have been working on it makes me smile really. When I was at school all I wanted to do was get out of it. The idea that one day I would write a book is crazy! And to imagine that I would be teaching – well now that really would knock my old teachers off their perches!

Many may say that the road I have travelled has been a pointless one, but the thing is - it is my road and every bump and twist and turn has been mine to look back on, and now to record for posterity. I suppose I would have been one of the scallies who would have nicked your gold teeth in days gone by, and at that time and in that place that would possibly have been my road.

I felt then that everything that I have done and all the decisions I have made have led to that point with Sammy and me. In her native Thai, Sammy's name means trade, but now I vowed the trade will stop. I wanted to walk with her on her road or mine from then on. We are probably very much alike, Sammy and I, in our own cultural contexts.

I loved waking up to the sweet scent of her lingering in the air, and I loved to see her eyes opening and looking at me with a deep and profound sincerity that made me think that there is some good in even the most evil corner of the world. I had no idea how long the scent of this wonderful girl will be with me, but I just could not bear to think of her being thrown back into the bear pit and used like an animal by men with no compassion. The men here really do not give a damn, life in the case of women like Sammy is cheap - she is totally expendable. There will be plenty more where she came from.

Sammy was sanity in my mad existence, the smell of bacon and eggs cooking in the morning and then being brought to me in bed, as though I was a prince, it was heaven!

That was until the police arrived banging down my door and looking for her. And so my life lurches on. But all I can say is the time I spent with Sammy gave a glimpse of what a loving and gentle life could be. Was I ready for such a life though?

* * *

It seems that whether I was ready for it or not, it was not to be! Sammy had gone. Another one bites the dust. I should have known better. I should know by now that you can never trust a hooker in any part of the world. However different you might think that, underneath it all they are all just the same. They are life's fuck ups.

I am amazed at how life can change in an instant. There I was with 5 visas and wondering if, after all, someone was looking down on me. I was almost 50 and I thought at last I knew what I wanted and if I had to fly all the way to China and back to find it, then that is what I would do.

The training continued and the landlord was still pissed off with me, but that was nothing new. If life has taught me one thing it is how different we all are. It would be pretty boring if we weren't, I suppose!

After all my efforts to save Sammy's sorry arse she went back on the game. I am beginning to wonder what it will take for me to find a decent woman; maybe I am trying too hard? Online there are thousands of Chinese putting themselves out there. For them once they are over 30 it is game over, no one wants them. I was talking to one who was 32 and retired, which makes me wonder where I went wrong or where she went right, how did she have the money to retire at 32? Probably better not to know!

In Ramadan things were quieter at work. It gave me time to think. Bad idea, I know! At the end of the day it does not matter if you are rich or poor, ugly or the most beautiful creature in the world; when your time is up and you get your ticket to heaven or hell it will all be the same for everyone.

All around you, all through your life, there will be people who think they know you, and don't. They think you don't know them when you do. There will be people always willing to talk up a storm about you behind your back.

Is what you become dependent on how you were brought up? I came from a very respectable family with the best mum and dad, so I should be sitting behind a desk pen pushing or something by now. But those of you who have been with me on this journey know that this is very far from how my life has panned out. My parents knew right from wrong and tried to teach it to me but I never listened. But to find myself teaching in the Middle East was a turn up for the books! My parents might have something to be proud of at last.

Now I am keen to pass on the experience I have had to those coming up behind me. My grandson - he will get the benefit of my wisdom and the way that things have been for me. God willing he will not make the mistakes that I have made. I cannot rewrite what has happened in my life but I can certainly pass on my experience to others and let them decide what seems like a better idea in life.

I have probably had undiagnosed mental issues, but whatever the case I am the proud father of three children, each with a different mother. I have never, as you have seen, had much luck with women; it starts well but soon goes downhill. I have always had visions of a dream family and, who knows, maybe one day I will get them.

* * *

I was paying way over the odds for my rent in the Middle East and the other day I was outside and caught short, so I had a piss in the sand. I looked over to my right and there was a bloke taking a dump! Dirty bugger!

The landlord thought he was really something very special but he did not mind his neighbour taking a dump al fresco so it is hardy the most elite of neighbourhoods.

That's not to say that on scaffolding jobs I have not been a little bit unorthodox in my toilet habits. I can remember once availing myself of a bucket in a garden when I needed to, with a tea towel off the line for bog roll! That was in Gloucester, not far from old Fred West's house of horrors.

I was looking at starting up my own scaffolding business in Saudi but it was a very complicated thing to do.

Health and safety was non-existent. One man dies – no probs, just buy another Indian - they are two a penny here.

Generally it seems that the world is pretty much fucked. We have scandal in governments and everyone looking after number one. Well I suppose I am stuck with the planet and it is stuck with me until I drop off my perch!

* * *

For my kids I want to say sorry that I was not there as much as I should have been and that I was not a better role model. Despite this, they have turned out great and I give their mother's credit for that. But they know that.

This is my story, Paul Scrase, Englishman, far from perfect - but still here!

Printed in Great Britain
by Amazon